Salt-Free Sauerkraut

FOR GOOD HEALTH!

Rich in Lactic Acid — the Great Detoxifier!

Learn How To Make This Wonderful Health Food
EASILY IN YOUR OWN KITCHEN!

WHAT THIS BOOK CAN DO FOR YOU . . .

You can feel better . . . look younger . . . feel stronger . . . have a sweet breath . . . and be vigorous regardless of your age! In fact, you may lead a healthy, active life to age 100 or more!

AWARENESS

The sun does not shine for a few trees
and flowers, but for the wide world's joy.

Henry Ward Beecher

To me, every hour of the day and night
is an unspeakably perfect miracle.

Walt Whitman

This world, after all our science
and sciences, is still a miracle,
wonderful, inscrutable, magical and more,
to whosoever will think of it.

Thomas Carlyle

There is nothing too little for so little a creature
as man. It is by studying little things that we attain
the great art of having as much happiness as possible.

Samuel Johnson

SALT FREE
HEALTH SAUERKRAUT
COOK BOOK

By Paul C. Bragg, N.D., Ph.D.

LIFE EXTENSION SPECIALIST

with

Patricia Bragg, Ph.D.

HEALTH AND BEAUTY CONSULTANT

Published by

HEALTH SCIENCE

Box 7, Santa Barbara, California 93102 U.S.A.

SALT FREE
HEALTH SAUERKRAUT
COOK BOOK

By

PAUL C. BRAGG, N.D., Ph.D.
Life Extension Specialist
with
PATRICIA BRAGG, Ph.D.
Health and Beauty Consultant

Copyright © Health Science

Eighth Printing   MCMLXXIX

Library of Congress Catalog Card Number: 74-32638
ISBN: 0-87790-025-6
Published by
HEALTH SCIENCE
Box 7, Santa Barbara, California 93102 U.S.A.

PRINTED IN THE UNITED STATES OF AMERICA

PAUL C. BRAGG
ON HIS RECENT ROUND-THE-WORLD LECTURE CRUSADE AT A
ROTORUA, NEW ZEALAND GREEN GROCERS PICKING FIRM,
GREEN CABBAGES FOR MAKING HIS SAUERKRAUT.

COURAGE

The greatest test of courage
on the earth is to bear defeat
without losing heart.

R. G. Ingersoll

Courage mounteth with occasion.

William Shakespeare

Courage is resistance to fear,
mastery of fear--
not absence of fear.

Mark Twain

What a new face courage
puts on everything!

Ralph Waldo Emerson

CONTENTS

Salt-Free Sauerkraut Recipes
From Around the World

FOR GOOD HEALTH!

CONTENTS (Continued)

MISS PATRICIA BRAGG
*Patricia enjoys preparing salt-free sauerkraut dishes for friends
when on world-wide lecture tours with her father, Paul C. Bragg.*

HAPPINESS

Learn the sweet magic of a cheerful face--
Not always smiling, but at least serene.

Oliver Wendell Holmes

Very little is needed to make a happy life.
It is all within yourself, in your way of thinking.

Marcus Aurelius

Happiness is but a name.

Robert Burns

Happiness is a habit--cultivate it.

Elbert Hubbard

The world is a looking glass,
and gives back to every man the reflection
of his own face. Frown at it, and it in turn
will look sourly upon you; laugh at it and with it,
and it is a jolly, kind companion.

William Makepeace Thackeray

Introduction
SAUERKRAUT'S LONG AND GLORIOUS HISTORY

By PATRICIA BRAGG
Nutritionist, Beauty and Physical Culture Specialist

People have been eating and enjoying the tangy taste of sauerkraut for many years. Not only have they enjoyed eating this delicious food, but they have gained the great health benefits that come with eating sauerkraut. It is a food that has proved itself for its tremendous health qualities.

SAUERKRAUT HELPED BUILD THE GREAT CHINA WALL

Sauerkraut dates back some 2000 years to Chinese Emperor Shih Huang-ti, who was responsible for the Great Wall of China. Without that fabulous Wall, we might have never have known the delightful goodness of sauerkraut. The toiling, slaving Chinese coolies, who built the monstrous structure, which snakes its way more than 1500 miles across Asia, were kept vigorous and strong by the cabbage used to supplement their diet of natural brown rice and soy beans. The cabbage was fermented with seeds of caraway, celery, dill and juniper berry and lo, a wonderful new taste was born. Sour and tasty to their liking.

Some thousand years later, the Great Wall notwithstanding, Genghis Khan plundered China. His tartar hordes took the fermented cabbage and added to their booty as they swept across Asia and Europe — they left a shamble of wrack and ruin and fermented cabbage.

The Germans fell in love with this piquant health food. Thus the Teutonic moniker for sauerkraut means "sour cabbage."

CAPTAIN COOK EXPLORED THE OCEANS ON SAUERKRAUT

Because it kept so well, sauerkraut was probably one of the first health foods to travel all-around the world. Captain James Cook, the great navigator, who discovered the Hawaiian Islands, credited his success in part to sauerkraut. A daily ration served his sailors prevented occurrence of the deadly, dreaded scurvy, long considered an unavoidable result of any long ocean voyage. Captain Cook probably learned the nutritional value of Sauerkraut from the writings of an English surgeon who attributed the absence of scurvy in the Dutch navy to the "zourkool" in their meals. He described it as "a meal of pickled cabbage" given them now and then. We know it today as "good old sauerkraut."

For one of Captain Cook's voyages in the unknown Pacific Ocean, he requisitioned almost 25,000 pounds of sauerkraut for the larders of two of his ships. The world would one day learn that it was not great seamanship or wizardry but ascorbic acid, or vitality vitamin C, in the sauerkraut that prevented the scurvy. Plus the friendly lactic acid micro-organisms called Lactobacillus acidophilus producing lactic acid ferments, which fight the unfriendly bacteria known as B. Coli. In Captain Cook's ship log of day by day happenings on board ship, he remarked about the splended health his crew enjoyed.

In due time, the Germans and the Holland Dutch who came to colonize the new world, brought with them their reputation, skill, and love of the marvelous pungent fermented cabbage.

Today, if you visit Eastern Pennsylvania, sauerkraut plays an important role in the lives and culture of the German and Dutch descendents of those early settlers.

My father and I have lectured in such cities as Lancaster, York, and Reading, Pennsylvania and sauerkraut is a daily food among many people. On the whole these people seem to enjoy robust health.

MODERN SCIENCE DISSECTS THE LOWLY SAUERKRAUT

Sauerkraut as I have stated is a perfect source of Vitality Vitamin C. Three-quarters of a cup provides about 25% of the daily minimum requirement for adults. Both B-1 and B-2, thiamine and riboflavin, are contained in sauerkraut. Vitamins C and B-1 must be replenished daily because neither is stored by the body. Sauerkraut's slight acidity provides natural protection against the destruction of the vitamins if it is cooked. Sauerkraut is also an economical and delicious source of calcium and phosphorous, and other important minerals, vitamins, enzymes and nutrients needed daily in the diet of both young and old alike.

Good health and good sense are two of life's greatest blessings.
Maxim 827 Pubilius Syrus

SAUERKRAUT — WEIGHT-WATCHER'S DELIGHT

It is a weight-watcher's delight. One cup of undrained sauerkraut contains only 33 calories; and a cup of sauerkraut juice has just 22 calories, putting both on the eat-as-much-as-you-want list for calorie counters.

It provides the intestines with the necessary bulk, moisture, and lubrication to assist one to have regular elimination.

Versatile sauerkraut is a boon to both regular eaters and weight-watchers; because it adds zest and goodness to meals in an endless number of tantalizing dishes, thereby preventing the monotony and helps the weak-willed not to falter in their calorie counting.

One of the highlights of my daily eating is to have a luscious tossed salad filled with freshly chopped or grated cabbage, carrots, celery, lettuce, cucumbers, green peppers, radishes and tomatoes . . . and I often top this mouth-watering salad with several tablespoons full of our home made salt-free sauerkraut. I often serve this to my dinner guests; and they seem to get great pleasure from this outstanding salad.

NORMAL INTESTINE: Salt-Free Sauerkraut is rich in lactic acid, which fights toxic poisons in intestines.

ABNORMAL INTESTINE: The result of intestinal toxemia. It is prolapsed and bloated.

To sum it all up salt-free sauerkraut is a perfect health food. It is bursting with valuable nutrients and it is not fattening. So for a slender, trim and slim figure, add salt-free sauerkraut to your daily menus. It's good; and good for you. So, put sauerkraut into your life.

FOOD FOR THOUGHT

The Great Sin — Fear

The Best Day — Today

The Best Town — Where You Succeed

The Best Work — What You Like

The Best Play — Work

The Greatest Stumbling Block — Egotism

The Greatest Mistake — Giving Up

The Most Expensive Indulgence — Hate

The Greatest Trouble-maker — One Who Talks Too Much

The Most Ridiculous Trait — False Pride

The Most Dangerous Man — The Liar

The Greatest Need — Common Sense

The Greatest Thought — God

The Greatest Wealth — Health

The Greatest Gift You Can Give or Receive — Love

The Greatest Race To Win — A Long Vigorous Life

Man's Greatest Companion and Friend — Good Books

Your Enemies — Envy, Greed, Self-Indulgence, Self-Pity

Life's Greatest Adventure — Growth on the Physical, Mental
and Spiritual Plane

Most Disgusting — A Show Off

Most Repulsive — A Bully

Most Overbearing Manner — Arrogance

Man's Greatest Stumbling Block — Ignorance

The Greatest Sieve — Before You Say Anything, Say To Yourself,
Is It Kind? — Is It True? — Is It Necessary

* THE CLEVEREST MAN *

ONE WHO ALWAYS DOES WHAT HE THINKS IS RIGHT

BE A CLEVER MAN!

SALT-FREE SAUERKRAUT

Nature's Perfect Health Food

For more than sixty years I have been an ardent research worker in the fields of Natural Nutrition and Naturopathy, including all branches of Health Culture such as scientific deep breathing, systematic exercise and physical therapy.

I love life . . . I am in love with life. By following the great laws of Nature I am today a great-grandfather with a painless, tireless and ageless body.

Most men of my calendar years have long ago died, and almost all the ones who remain are only half alive . . . living in complete senility . . . human vegetables.

DON'T GET CAUGHT IN THE "AGE TRAP"

Most humans get caught in the "age trap," because they believe that time is a destroyer of youth, health and life. They believe that the longer they live the more they deteriorate mentally and physically. They blame the years for their failing eyes, unsteady nerves and poor memory. To them, all their ailments have been loaded upon them by the years they have lived. They believe that time is an evil force which turns them into physical wrecks.

Don't you believe it! Time is not a force . . . time is simply a measure.

Man lives by the law of compensation. If you obey the laws of Nature in regard to your eating and living habits, you will be rewarded with radiant, vigorous health at any age. Just remember that what you sow in one period of your life, you reap in the other. Don't blame the years for your poor health . . . blame your ignorance of how to live healthfully.

It was Confucius who said: "Eat not for the pleasure thou mayest find therein; eat to increase thy strength, eat to preserve the life thou has received from Heaven."

People who are plagued with stiff joints, aching feet and muscles, lack of energy and a general rundown condition brought this condition upon themselves.

People who live by knowledge and wisdom are rewarded with a long and healthful life.

HILDEGARDE OF BINGEN (1098-1180), almost a thousand years ago wrote:

"I am that living and fiery essence of the divine substance that glows in the beauty of the fields. I shine in the water, I burn in the sun and moon and the stars . . . I breathe in the verdure and in the flowers, and when the waters flow like living things, it is I . . . I am Wisdom. Mine is the blast of the thundered Word by which all things were made . . . I am life."

The universe itself does not hold life cheaply. Life as we know it appears to be a rare occurrence among the billions of galaxies and solar systems that occupy space. As far as we have yet determined in this particular system, human life occurs on only this one planet. Of all the countless forms of life on this planet Earth, only one . . . the human species . . . possesses the combination of certain faculties which give it supreme advantages over all the others. Among those faculties or gifts is a creative intelligence that enables man to reflect, anticipate and speculate, to encompass past experience and visualize future needs.

Knowledge is power! The more we can learn about making our bodies healthier, stronger and more youthful, the longer we are going to live.

LACTIC ACID VITAL TO HEALTH

Some of this knowledge is so simple and basic that it tends to be overlooked or ignored. We become dazzled with space exploration and the "magic" of sophisticated computers.

But man has yet to discover all the "magic" of his own body. No computer yet devised . . . or likely to be for a long, long time . . . can equal the intricate, living mechanism of the human body.

A fight for life and death is going on in your body this very moment as you read this book. It is taking place in your lower intestine . . . between the friendly bacteria that fight disease and putrefaction, and the unfriendly bacteria that produce poisons which permeate your entire system and cause a toxic condition.

2

If you are well and healthy, if you have a clear skin, a sparkling youthful eye, good muscle tone, a spring in your step and a glow to your complexion, if you are free from bad breath and body odor and feel full of vim and vigor, you have a preponderance of friendly bacteria in your lower bowel.

These friendly bacteria are fed on lactic acid. If your supply of lactic acid is deficient, then the unfriendly bacteria holds your body in their deathly grip.

Putrefactive decaying bacteria in the lower bowel is your greatest enemy. They can cause a condition known as autointoxication, or self-poisoning. When you are in the vicious grip of auto-intoxication your physical troubles begin. The headaches, the stiff joints, the dead tired feeling, the sleeplessness, the poor complexion, the dead-looking hair, the bleeding gums, the plugged sinus cavities, the post-nasal drip of phlegm in your throat, the lifeless eyes, the bad breath and body odor, the washed-out feeling, the lack of interest in life . . . can all be due to a deficiency in lactic acid. Lack of this important nutrient . . . vital ammunition for the friendly bacteria . . . means that vile toxic poisons go into your bloodstream and into your vital organs and every one of the billions of cells that make up your body. Boils, tumors, adverse skin conditions, are all signs that the body has been taken over by these toxic poisons.

Lactic acid feeds the friendly bacteria, and gives them the strength to detoxify your body. They are powerful when supplied with lactic acid. They are your security for abundant living. They are your life-savers.

Why do lactic acid ferments contribute to youth and vitality well into the sunset years? Lactic acid is necessary for the vitality and growth of new cells — the very seeds of life. Each little cell in your body is constantly engaged in the life-renewal process of taking in food and oxygen and throwing off waste products. This process depends on the presence of certain lactic acid ferments.

The East European peoples known for their enviable record of longevity have to thank lactic acid for their excellent health and youthful vitality. Their diets, are high in soured foods — rich in lactic acid such as sour milk, yogurt, black sour-dough bread, sauerkraut and the like. Lactic acid has a beneficial anti-putre-factive effect on the intestines and keeps the digestive tract in good health.

Besides eating a wide variety of fresh raw foods, primitive people usually included a staple ferment in their daily menu. The Eskimos had their own way of making sauerkraut, the South Sea Islanders eat fermented Taro flour called Poi; in Africa a drink is fermented from millet.

These "primitive" people enjoy exceptional health and vitality, practically no dental caries and practically none of the degenerative diseases that take such a disastrous toll of those of us who live in "civilized" societies.

LIFE'S GREATEST TREASURE IS RADIANT HEALTH

"There is no substitute for Health. Those who possess it are richer than kings."

SAUERKRAUT — A PRIME SOURCE OF LACTIC ACID

Sauerkraut . . . especially the Salt-Free Sauerkraut which is the subject of this book . . . is rich in lactic acid. Sauerkraut is not only a naturally fermented food but rich in vitamin C and in Enzymes because the cabbage is not subjected to heat. Commercial sauerkrauts are usually preserved with benzoate of soda which is harmful, and loaded with salt which is also harmful.

That is why this book is so important to you. It will tell you how to make this wonderful health Sauerkraut in your own kitchen . . . how to serve it in attractive appetizing ways, so that your entire family will enjoy eating it, and will help add to your good health as a result. Salt-free sauerkraut has a beneficial, anti-putrefactive effect on the intestines. It helps to keep the digestive tract in good health . . . and that is where the good health of the whole body begins.

Salt-free sauerkraut is an essential part of the Natural Nutritional Program outlined in this book. If you follow this program, you will really set your feet on the Royal Road to Health.

NATURAL NUTRITION MUST RULE YOUR DIET

Eating salt-free sauerkraut must be part of a diet that is based on natural nutrition, free from dead and embalmed foods. You cannot eat any old kind of refined, processed foods and expect even the marvelous salt-free sauerkraut to perform miracles. Nature does not work that way.

You must abandon refined white sugar and its products . . . You must stop coffee, tea and alcohol from entering your body . . . You must eat no chemicalized foods such as hot dogs, luncheon meats, ham, bacon . . . You must not poison yourself with products contaminated with chemical additives . . . You must eliminate commercial dry cereals and white rice . . . You must not use commercial saturated fat foods . . . And you must live on a completely salt-free diet.

To get the full benefit of salt-free sauerkraut you must eat live foods. Three-fifths of your diet must be composed of fresh fruit and vegetables . . . plenty of raw fruit and vegetable salads . . . plenty of properly cooked vegetables. (I use nothing frozen, or canned for most canned foods have additives — sugar, salt, etc.)

One-fifth of your diet must be composed of good healthy protein such as soy beans, raw nuts and seeds (if one has difficulty chewing nuts and seeds, then grind them as needed) . . . natural, unprocessed cheese (if milk products agree with you — for some it causes mucus) . . . lean meats free of chemically fattening hormones . . . properly fed poultry . . . fresh, fertile eggs . . . brewers yeast and raw wheat germ.

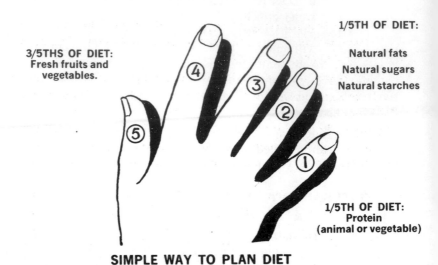

3/5THS OF DIET:
Fresh fruits and
vegetables.

1/5TH OF DIET:

Natural fats
Natural sugars
Natural starches

1/5TH OF DIET:
Protein
(animal or vegetable)

SIMPLE WAY TO PLAN DIET

The final fifth of the natural diet consists of natural sweets such as honey and 100% maple syrup . . . sun-dried fruits — only those free of all preserving chemicals — such as dates, figs, raisins, apricots, peaches, prunes, apples . . . natural starches such as whole grains, brown rice, beans, lentils . . . and natural, unsaturated oils such as soy oil, olive oil, sunflower seed oil, sesame oil, peanut oil and corn oil. These oils should be purchased at your Health Food Store, so you can be sure they are cold pressed.

Now, with a Nutritional Health Program composed of live natural foods . . . plus your Salt-Free Sauerkraut . . . you are really going to see constructive things happen in your body. You are now working WITH Nature, not against it!

Here is a health program understandable to all open-minded, thinking people. It is a simplified program, which attacks the basic causes of human miseries. You are what you eat! Live on a diet of natural foods, and keep the friendly bacteria in your lower intestine strong and active.

People who live by knowledge and wisdom are the ones who can help themselves regain and maintain a strong, healthy body.

6

A SEARCH FOR THE SECRET OF LIFE

It was a beautiful day at Leysin, Switzerland. The mountains surrounding this beauty spot were covered with snow. The whole world looked bright and clean.

I was ready to leave Dr. August Rollier's great Natural Healing and Sun Sanatorium. I was completely cured from a case of T.B. that had almost cost me my life. I felt reborn. No longer were my lungs the victim of T.B. germs. I was not an arrested case . . . mine was a complete cure. I had been cured by natural foods, clean air and powerful solar rays. I was just eighteen years of age.

There were tears in my eyes as I stood beside Dr. Rollier. This man had taken me in a condition which I and all my family and friends had considered hopeless . . . and had restored me to a normal, healthy life. It was a sad parting, but I no longer needed the great doctor's services. He had finished his work with me, and I was a completely new person. But it was difficult for me to say good-bye to the man who had transformed me from a lung cripple into a strong athlete. I loved him as a son would love a devoted father.

The good doctor put his strong arm around my waist and asked, "Paul, what are your plans for life?"

I answered, "Doctor, when I was the sickest a human could be, I made a promise that whatever system cured me of my death-dealing T.B., that system of healing would be the one I would follow as my life's career. I was cured by a drugless method of healing at your sanatorium. Therefore, my studies will be natural healing in all its branches . . . biochemistry, nutrition, physical education and physical therapy . . . and a thorough course in the Naturopathic method. But first I have some practical research to do."

"Dr. Rollier," I said, "I am on the quest to learn the secret of life. I know it is a tremendous undertaking, but I am determined to pursue this research. Now that I am well again, I want to extend my life to as many years as I can. I would like to live at least 120 years. That is my goal."

And I told the good doctor that not only his treatment but his library had set my feet on the road to that goal.

METCHNIKOFF'S THEORY OF AUTOINTOXICATION

During the two years that I was a patient at Dr. Rollier's Sanitorium, I had studied many of the books in his extensive library. The great Russian Scientist, Professor Elie Metchnikoff, had fascinated me with his theory that all diseases of the human body may be caused by autointoxication. His theory is that the difference between buoyant health and disease depends largely upon the predominance of one or another type of bacterial action in the food residue which reaches the large intestine.

Metchnikoff went so far as to declare that old age and senility are attributable to poisonous toxins that cause hardening of the arteries and many other degenerative diseases. These toxins, he said, arise from the colon, due to the action of putrefactive bacteria (B. Coli), called unfriendly bacteria.

In health, these putrefactive bacteria are held in check by friendly lactic acid micro-organisms, called Lactobacillus acidophilus, which produce lactic acid ferments detrimental to the B. Coli.

Metchnikoff's theory was based upon the extensive research he had done among certain people of Russia and the Austria-Hungarian Empire (now known as Yugoslavia). Metchnikoff reported that these people enjoy a superior state of health, living active, vigorous, robust lives up to 100 years of age. In fact, he found that more people in this area lived to 100 years or more than anywhere else in the world. They were exceptionally strong and virile, the men fathering children up to age 90 and sometimes older. They were great mountain climbers, with tremendous endurance. They had no arthritis, practically no dental caries, and rarely suffered from degenerative diseases.

SALT-FREE SAUERKRAUT — STAPLE DIET OF THESE VIGOROUS PEOPLE

According to Metchnikoff, there are many factors which make these people so healthy and long-lived. He felt that one of the most important was the eating of foods rich in lactic acid. Their meals included all kinds of soured foods, high in lactic acid content, such as yoghurt, sour milk and black sourdough bread. But Metchnikoff found that the finest source of lactic acid in the diet of these vigorous people was their home-made salt-free sauerkraut. It was this staple of their diet, he stated, that produced the greatest amount of friendly bacteria in the intestines. One of the cases Metchnikoff cited was that of a Russian who was 143 years of age, and who had perfect vision, an alert mind and a robust body. He ate home-made salt-free sauerkraut daily. Another case was a woman in Austria who was a mountain guide at the age of 101. She was not only a vigorous woman, but also had a natural beauty that attracted men. Several times a day she ate salt-free sauerkraut, and carried a jar of it in her pack sack when mountain climbing.

I VERIFY METCHNIKOFF'S RESEARCH

When I was ready to leave Dr. Rollier's Sanatorium at age 18, I determined that my first research into the secret of longevity would be to live among and study the vigorous people whom Metchnikoff had written about. I bid Dr. Rollier good-bye, and set out on my first research adventure. My pack-sack carried all my gear . . . my sleeping bag, extra wearing apparel, eating equipment, and some staple foods such as nuts, raisins, seeds and dates.

The mighty Swiss Alps tower around Leysin, Switzerland, which itself is a mile above sea level. Breathing deeply of the clean, invigorating air, I set off down the long mountain trail toward my destination. After a long journey, I arrived in the Balkan Penninsula in Southeast Europe, east of Italy.

At last I was in the very area where Metchnikoff made his greatest discoveries about the health qualities of foods rich in lactic acid. Just look at your map of today's Yugoslavia, and you will locate where I was. This was a wild and primitive section at that time, more than seventy years ago. Cities were few and far between.

I had never seen such healthy, vigorous people as I found there. And I never saw a person there wearing glasses, using a hearing aid, carrying crutches or using a cane . . . in fact, not even limping.

I was very lucky in finding a guide, Andrei, who spoke English as well as nine of the languages and dialects used in that area including Slovak, Czech, Slovene, Serbo-Croatian, Bulgarian and Slavonic. He was a powerfully built man who appeared to be about sixty years old. When he revealed his age as 89, I could hardly believe it. His eyes were clear and sparkling, his body was strong and healthy, his mind keen and sharp. He was a kindly and happy man. He had a fine, resonant voice. And he ate salt-free sauerkraut daily, and had a great faith in its health qualities.

Andrei knew every part of this area, and served as my guide, interpreter and congenial companion during my travels and research which lasted more than a year. I kept a daily journal with a detailed account of everything that happened, everyone I saw, and especially what they ate and how they lived. At this very moment I have the yellowed, faded journal before me, so I can give you an accurate account of this eventful journey of discovery.

METCHNIKOFF'S THEORIES PRACTICAL

I found every word which Metchnikoff wrote about these amazing people to be absolutely true. Here indeed were human beings of superior health. In the hundreds of miles which my guide Andrei and I traveled, I never encountered a bald-headed man . . . I met no fat, overweight men or women. I could not have actually believed it if I had not seen it with my own eyes that one could find such healthy, youthful, strong, happy, long-lived people. There was no T.B., which had almost taken my life . . . no degenerative diseases.

I lived with these people for more than a year. Their diet included a wide variety of fresh, raw foods. They all had tremendous gardens . . . plenty of fresh fruit grew on their trees. Their diet was also rich in fermented lactic acid foods, particularly salt-free sauerkraut, sour milk, yoghurt and black sourdough bread.

I realized that Metchnikoff was correct in attributing the perpetual youthfulness of these people to the preponderance of these lactic acid foods in their daily diet. He said that lactic acid is absolutely necessary for the vitality and growth of new body cells . . . which he called "the very seeds of life" . . . because each tiny cell in the body is constantly engaged in the life-renewal process of taking in food and oxygen and throwing off toxic wastes. This vital process depends upon the presence of certain lactic acid ferments.

Now remember, these people of Southeast Europe ate naturally fermented foods. No additives, no chemicals, no commercial poisons. Their staple, salt-free sauerkraut, was not only naturally fermented and therefore rich in lactic acid . . . but it was also rich in vitality vitamin C as well as important enzymes.

These people lived the simple, basic health life in every way. They took plenty of vigorous exercise in the pure, fresh air. They went to bed early and were up with the dawn. Not only did they have healthy bodies . . . they were also happy and contented, enjoying peace of mind and calm nerves.

I encountered no one with heart trouble, no one who had suffered a stroke.

THESE VIGOROUS PEOPLE USED NO SALT

I am sure that one of the main reasons why these wonderful folk of Southeastern Europe, in the beautiful Balkan penninsula, suffered no heart disease or strokes was because they used absolutely no salt in their diet. None of the babies or children ever contracted rheumatic fever, a severe disease of our present civilization which frequently causes permanent damage to the heart valves.

Doctors were few and far between in this primitive area. Most of their practice consisted of delivering babies and taking care of injuries in accidents. Those with whom I had conferences told me that constipation and intestinal ills were unknown.

One of the doctors with whom I spent a great deal of time had worked with Metchnikoff while he was doing his research in this area. This doctor, who himself was a splendid specimen of a man, told me that in his forty years of general practice he had never seen a patient with a rupture or piles. Ulcers were absolutely unknown. He agreed with Metchnikoff that the natural, salt-free, high lactic acid diet helped safeguard these people from intestinal troubles and degenerative diseases.

The doctor had great esteem for Metchnikoff as a scientist, and praised the thoroughness of his research. He said that Metchnikoff, like myself, thoroughly enjoyed the salt-free sauerkraut, and that the scientist strongly opposed the use of salt in the human diet.

11

Medical and scientific research today . . . spurred on by the high incidence of high blood pressure and fatal heart diseases . . . is substantiating the basic wisdom of a natural, salt-free diet.

TODAY'S NO. 1 KILLER — HEART DISEASE

Heart disease accounts for 54% of all the deaths in the United States today, according to a recent report by the National Health Education Committee. This No. 1 Killer claimed 1,505,380 lives last year. Some 24% of these victims were between the ages of 25 and 64, in the prime of life.

The main cause of heart disease is arteriosclerosis or hardening of the arteries.

Our bloodstream is our stream of life, carrying oxygen and food to every one of the billions of cells in our body and carrying away the waste products of cell metabolism. When the heart sends the blood pulsing through the body, the naturally strong and elastic walls of the arteries keep this stream of life going.

But the blood can only carry what we put into our body. When we contaminate our bloodstream with inorganic minerals, we are committing slow suicide. Our body chemistry cannot digest or assimilate such minerals, so these hard crystals are deposited in our vital organs, causing kidney stones and gallstones . . . and particularly on the walls of the arteries, becoming imbedded in the tissue and making it hard and brittle. Gradually the elasticity of the arterial walls is destroyed. No longer is the blood vigorously aided on its journey . . . on the contrary, it is impeded, and the pressure against the brittle, inelastic arterial walls causes further injury . . . until finally the wall breaks and the blood hemmorhages into adjacent organs or tissues.

When this occurs in a cardiac (heart) artery, a heart attack or heart failure can result . . . in the brain, a paralytic stroke.

Damaging inorganic minerals often enter the body in "hard" water . . . we can literally drink ourselves to death on water! (See my book, "The Shocking Truth About Water," for details.)

But by far the worst culprit . . . the real assassin . . . is ordinary table salt.

God makes all things good; man meddles with them and they become evil.
—Rousseau

12

SALT LINKED TO HIGH BLOOD PRESSURE

Reporting on recent research showing a definite relationship between salt intake and hypertension (high blood pressure), writer Frank Maier of Newsweek Feature Service headed his article:

SALT OR NOT?
CAUTION: Salt May Be Hazardous To Your Health

"Will that be the salt-shaker warning of the future? (The article continued.) It could be, if some medical researchers have their way.

"For after years of research, scientists claim to be discerning a relationship between the consumption of salt and hypertension (or high blood pressure), an affliction suffered by 8.8 million Americans and that often leads to strokes and heart disease."

"According to Dr. Lewis K. Dahl, chief of staff of the Medical Research Center at Brookhaven National Laboratory, Upton, New York, the first evidence against salt came from studies of hypertension among Eskimos, Marshall Islanders, North Americans, Southern Japanese and Northern Japanese. *The Northern Japanese, with the saltiest diet of those studied, had the highest incidence of hypertension."

"If the primary evidence was circumstantial, subsequent studies have offered more concrete proof. During a period of years, 30,000 laboratory rats were fed varying salt diets and, says Dahl, those with high-salt diets showed 'a classic response.'

" 'We've had people lose 50 to 75 pounds but with no loss of high blood pressure,' he said, 'unless we also reduced their salt intake.'

" 'A person who eats the normal diet consumes about five grams of salt a day,' said Dahl, 'even if he doesn't add salt at the table. This is five to ten times as much as his body needs by metabolic standards . . . Salt is put into baby food only for the sake of the mothers: Mother tastes to see if the baby will like it, so the

*(NOTE: Here in Hawaii, where I am writing this book, we have thousands of Japanese, among whom we find a very high incidence of high blood pressure. The Japanese use monosodium glutamate and large amounts of table salt in the preparation of their foods, then add soy sauce which contains 36% pure salt.)

baby-food manufacturers make sure Mother likes it. But the fact is that baby doesn't need it.' "

(NOTE: Giving the baby salted food starts it on its way to heart disease, high blood pressure and strokes. No wonder 52% of all deaths in the U.S.A. are caused by heart disease!)

SALT IS A POISON

Would you use sodium, a caustic alkali, to season your food? Or chlorine, a poisonous gas? "Ridiculous questions," you say. "Nobody could be foolhardy enough to do that."

Of course not — knowingly. But the shocking truth is that most people do use these two poisons in their food . . . because they don't know that these powerful chemicals constitute the inorganic crystaline compound known as SALT!

Yes, that's right. Common, ordinary table salt is a poison. For centuries, the expression "salt of the earth" has been used as a catch-all phrase to designate something good and essential. But nothing could be farther from the truth.

That "harmless" product, sodium chloride, that you shake into your food every day may actually bury you!

SALT IS NOT A FOOD

There is no more justification for the use of sodium chloride as a food than there is for using potassium chloride, calcium chloride, barium chloride, or any other strong chemical on the druggist's shelf.

Salt has no nutritional value . . . no vitamins . . . no organic minerals . . . no nutrients of any kind! Does this shock you? Here's more:

Salt cannot be digested, assimilated or utilized by the human body. On the contrary, it is actually harmful. It may bring on troubles in the kidneys, bladder, gall bladder, heart, arteries and veins. Salt may waterlog the tissues, causing a dropsical condition.

Salt may act as a heart poison. It also increases the irritability of the nervous system.

Salt acts to rob calcium from the body. It attacks the mucus lining throughout the entire gastrointestinal tract.

14

It is not only harmful to humans. Salt acts as a positive poison to the lower animals as well, particularly to fowl and swine. Even salt water fish cannot live in water that has too great a concentration of salt. Intensive government research is now underway to find a method to reduce and control the salt content of California's Salton Sea, which is nearing the saturation limit for sustaining fish or other marine life. If something is not done soon it will become another Dead Sea, like the famous one in the Holy Land which derived its name from the fact that it contains no life of any kind.

Plants, which are the only organisms that can convert inorganic minerals into organic, can also be killed by an oversaturation of salt. This has become a major problem in farmlands dependent upon irrigation, where water deposits salt into the soil.

HOW DID THE SALT HABIT ORIGINATE?

If salt is so dangerous to health, why is it used so widely?* Mainly because it is a habit that has become ingrained over thousands of years, dating from the time that man first discovered that salt (which acts as a preservative) would keep meat and other foods from spoiling. The fact that salt acted as a quick poison to the putrefactive bacteria in meat and other foods was considered a blessing . . . without thought that this same chemical compound might also act as a slow poison to the human body. Of course, our remote ancestors who first discovered salt as a preservative did not know or try to analyze why it acted as such. Without refrigeration or other means of preserving food, they salted it, especially meat. Salt became such an habitual part of man's diet that he accepted it as a food.

There is a natural craving in the human body for organic sodium. The biochemist, Bunge, explains that in prehistoric times there was a proper balance of sodium and potassium minerals in the earth, which were transmuted by plants into organic form digestible by animals including man. But as man developed the cultivation of crops, clearing land, continued rainfall over the centuries washed away the more soluble sodium salts. In time,

*(NOTE: I wonder this about other unhealthy items sold and used by millions — coffee, china tea, smoking, self drugs, chemicalized foods, etc.)

some soils and land-grown foods became deficient in sodium but high in potassium. The result was that animals and human beings developed a craving for something to replace this deficiency. They found an ineffective and highly dangerous substitute in inorganic sodium chloride, or common salt.

That the salt habit is unnatural is attested to by the fact that many primitive people do not use salt. The native Eskimos, for example, although their diet consisted largely of meat and fish, were able to preserve their food with natural ice and enjoyed it without salt. As civilization has encroached upon these people, the Eskimo has been victimized by the white man's poisons — including salt — as have other native peoples, with a consequent decline and deterioration in health.

EFFECT OF SALT ON THE BODY

Swallowing salt to obtain natural sodium is like taking inorganic calcium to get calcium. It is as ineffective and far more harmful than sucking on a tenpenny nail to obtain organic iron!

Inorganic chemicals cannot be assimilated by body cells, and they are actually harmful to the digestive organs. The stomach develops a sudden and abnormal thirst after salt is consumed . . . a natural reaction to wash a foreign substance out of the body.

You can imagine what an effect this has on the delicate kidney filters. Of all the body organs, the kidneys are most subject to injury from salt.

What happens when more salt is eaten than the kidneys can eliminate? The excess is deposited in various tissues of the body, especially in the feet and lower legs. To protect the tissues against this poison — salt — the body automatically seeks to dilute it by accumulating water in these areas. As the tissues become waterlogged, they tend to swell. Feet and ankles bloat painfully. When these areas have reached their saturation point, the salt and resultant waterlogging is deposited in other tissues, then in the vital organs.

The ultimate result is extreme shortness of breath due to excess fluid in the lungs . . . and finally congestive heart failure. The action of the heart muscle is governed by the relative concentration and balance of natural, organic sodium and calcium in the blood. An excess of sodium will tend to disturb this action, increasing the heartbeat and the blood pressure. This creates the demand for more oxygen, which waterlogged lungs cannot supply . . . and puts increased demand on a heart already burdened with fluid in its own tissues. The heart cannot cope, so it stops beating.

As already noted, salt is a major contributing factor to high blood pressure, or hypertension, with its resultant diseases and death.

THE MYTH OF THE "SALT LICK"

Even with the accumulating evidence in favor of a salt-free diet, there are still some die-hard defenders of salt who claim that a salt-free diet is a deficient diet. They cite the fact that even wild animals will travel miles to visit so-called "salt-licks."

I have investigated numbers of these "salt-licks" where wild animals congregate to lick the soil. The one chemical property which all such salt-licks had in common was **the complete absence of sodium chloride!** There was an abundance of many organic minerals which the animals craved . . . but absolutely NO organic or inorganic sodium at these natural salt licks.

As to the artificial salt-licks or large blocks of salt used by cattle raisers and dairy farmers, these serve a definite commercial purpose. It may be, of course, that the owners really believe that the cattle need salt. The practical result, however, is that licking the salt blocks makes the cattle thirsty, and they drink a great deal of water. In the case of beef cattle, which are sold by weight, the water adds profitable pounds. On a dairy farm, the more water the cows drink the more milk produced.

The excess salt content is passed along to human consumers. Commercial milk, for example, has been found to contain the very high ratio of 1½ grams of salt per quart. For a five-month-old infant, this proportion is equivalent to ½ ounce of salt to an adult.

As previously noted, babies not only do not need salt . . . it is dangerous in their diet. It is my opinion that obese, unhealthy infants and children . . . and there are all too many of them in our affluent America . . . are the victims of salted foods. They

17

are heavy drinkers of commercial milk, and most of their foods are saturated with salt . . . canned and bottled foods, cheese, bread, practically everything that comes from the supermarkets.

THE FALLACY OF SALT TABLETS

The myth of the human need for salt persists throughout life. We are told, for example, that salt tablets should be taken in hot weather to compensate the body for salt lost by perspiring. In my opionion, this is not only fallacious . . . it is dangerous.

To prove my point, I made a test myself in Death Valley, California, one of the hottest locations in the world and at its hottest in July and August. It was here that I staged a test hike of 30 miles from Furnace Creek Ranch to Stovepipe Wells at the end of July. I hired ten husky young college athletes to make this hike with me.

An accompanying jeep was loaded with both cold and warm water, salt tablets, and plenty of food such as the young men wanted — bread, buns, crackers, cheese, lunch meats, hot dogs, cola drinks on ice.

We started the hike about 8 a.m., with the thermometer at 105 degrees. The higher the sun rose, the more cruel the heat became . . . up and up went the thermometer until at 12 noon it stood at 130 degrees . . . a dry, sizzling heat.

The college boys gobbled salt tablets and guzzled cool water along the way . . . and at noon lunch they ate ham and cheese sandwiches washed down with ice-cold cola drinks.

As for great-grandfather Paul Bragg . . . I was on a complete fast, except for drinking warm distilled water as I needed it.

We rested a half-hour after lunch, then continued our rugged hike across the blazing hot sands. Soon things began to happen to the strong, husky college boys. First, three of them got violently ill and threw up all they had eaten and drank for lunch . . . they got dizzy and turned deathly pale, and were overcome with weakness. They quit the hike cold, and were driven back to the Furnace Creek Ranch.

The hike continued with seven college athletes and me. As we hiked, they drank large amounts of cold water and took salt tablets. Then suddenly five of them got stomach cramps and became quite ill. Up came the water and some of the lunch . . . and these five had to be driven back to the ranch.

That left only two of the boys . . . and myself. It was now about 4 p.m., and the merciless sun beat down upon us with great fury. Almost to the second, the last remaining salt-tablet athletes collapsed in the hot sun onto the burning sand . . . and had to be rushed back to the ranch for medical care.

That left great-grandfather Bragg alone on the test . . . and I felt fresh as a daisy! I was not full of salt tablets and I was not full of food. The only thing I had put into my stomach since morning was the warm distilled water.

I finished the 30-mile desert hike in about 10½ hours . . . and I had no ill effects whatsoever! I camped out for the night . . . then arose before dawn the next morning and hiked another 30 miles back to the ranch . . . without food or salt tablets.

The medical doctors gave me a thorough examination and found me in perfect condition.

No salt tablets were supplied to Rommel's famous German-Afrikan Corps in its sweep across Egypt and subsequent retreat from El Alamein across hundreds of miles of blazing desert . . . yet the British found the captured Nazi troops in good physical condition.

Many experiments performed with humans on a non-salt diet under hot desert conditions confirm my own Death Valley test.

According to scientific studies, what happens is this: After the first few days of acclimatization, the subjects cease to lose sodium through perspiration. Apparently there is a normalizing body mechanism which conserves sodium in the body.

Under all ordinary weather conditions, people on rigid salt-free diets show comfortable endurance. This also tends to confirm that the so-called need for added salt in hot weather has been greatly exaggerated.

Nature never deceives us; it is always we who deceive ourselves.   Rousseau

---

Personal beauty is a greater recommendation than any letter of introduction.
                                                                      Aristotle

WHAT IS THE BODY'S SALT TOLERANCE?

There has been a great deal of research on the amount of salt which the human body can tolerate. In the opinion of research scientists, the daily salt tolerance of the body varies from ½ to 1 gram per day.

The average American actually consumes 15 to 30 times his salt tolerance each day!

This unfortunately high figure is due primarily to the excessive amount of "hidden salt" in almost all commercially prepared foods. It is in bread, cheese, prepared meats (ham, bacon, lunch meats, etc.), canned vegetables, and hundreds of other staple foods. Added to this is the habit of most people to season all fresh meats and vegetables with salt . . . adding insult to injury!

The Southern Negroes have the highest blood pressure of any group in the United States. Data indicates that, for most of them, salt is a prominent item in their diet, salted pork being one of their main staples.

Southern whites have a similar problem. I was born and reared in Virginia, and many of my relatives suffered from high blood pressure. They died early of strokes and kidney diseases, chiefly because they were heavy eaters of salt pork, ham and bacon. High concentrations of salt were used at every meal. By the time these people were thirty years old, they ached all over with what they called "the misery." Their joints became cemented, and they hobbled around stiffly and painfully. It is my opinion that the heavy salt diet of the average Southerner is to blame for such "misery."

The most dramatic case of salt injury occurred not long ago in a Binghamton, N.Y. hospital, where a number of babies died when salt was inadvertently used in their formula. An overdose of salt can kill a baby quickly.

The laws of health are inexorable; we see people going down and out in the prime of life simply because no attention is paid to them. *Bragg*

Simplicity . . . simplicity . . . simplicity, let your affairs be as two or three, and not as a hundred or a thousand.

DE-SALTING THE BODY BY FASTING

If you have been eating the average American diet, you have accumulated an excess of salt in your system. How can you get rid of this deadly poison?

Your body is a marvelous self-regulating mechanism. It is self-repairing and self-healing . . . if you give it a chance, Nature's way. Nature's method of de-toxifying the body is by fasting.

I have had more than fifty years experience with the science and use of rational fasting. And I have found that in four days of complete fasting, we can de-salt the body.

By complete fasting, I mean that for four entire 24-hour days nothing must pass through your body but distilled water. You may drink all the distilled water you want — but you must not drink or eat anything else.

As a record of how this 4-day fast will cleanse your body of salt, each morning take a sample of the first urine the body passes. Put this bottle of urine up on a shelf and let it cool and settle for two or three weeks. Then take it out in the sunlight and look at it . . . you will see the concentrated sodium chloride in the bottom of the bottle along with other morbid body wastes.

The first thing the body throws off during a fast is salt, and the bloat that goes with it. Lumpy, waterlogged spots vanish . . . your body becomes more streamlined. Bloat is gone and you begin to see your natural figure again.

Notice, too, how freely the kidneys will function . . . notice how naturally moist your mouth is . . . how you have no abnormal thirst. Notice your skin tone, your muscle tone . . . the thinner and more youthful look to your entire body.

You can hardly believe your eyes . . . a wonderful transformation is taking place during your fast. The powerful "Vital Force" that would otherwise be used to handle your food is now being used exclusively to clean out the debris, the waste, the poisons that have been locked in the body cells and vital organs. The rejuvenation is taking place in every one of the billions of cells of your body!

Perfect health is above gold, and a sound body before riches. *Solomon*

After the four days of de-salting the body by this complete distilled water fast, KEEP SALT OUT OF YOUR BODY! It is a difficult thing to do, because of the "hidden salt" in so many of our foods. That is why I recommend a 24-hour fast every week to help you de-salt weekly.

As I travel over the world lecturing and doing research, I often find it difficult to avoid "hidden salt" in foods . . . even though I always request "No salt, please," in restaurants, on steamships, trains and airplanes. However, I feel that my weekly 24-hour fast keeps the inorganic salt flowing out of my body.

There is never any salt added to my food. There is no salt ever used in the Bragg household! We season with herbs, kelp seasoning and garlic, which are the real, natural seasonings. They will put zest in your foods. (Consult my books, "The Miracle of Fasting" and "The Four-Generation Health Cook Book" to help you with this program.)

With fasting and a low-salt diet, see for yourself how much better you will feel and look! And what a sweet taste you will always have in your mouth. You will note many other changes for the better when you fast and banish salt from your diet.

NATURAL SODIUM SUPPLIED BY NATURAL FOODS

The body needs natural sodium — organic sodium, not table salt, an inorganic chemical. You can obtain natural sodium which Nature provides in organic form from such vegetables as beets, celery, carrots, potatoes, turnips, sea vegetation, kelp, water-cress, and many other natural foods. Remember, the organic mineral is the only such substance that can be utilized by your living cells.

There is actually enough natural sodium in fresh vegetables, fish, meats and other natural foods to supply all the needed organic sodium required by your body.

Proof of this fact is found in the known past history of many people throughout the world who never used salt. The American Indians, for example, knew nothing about salt before the first foreign explorers arrived. Columbus and all of the other great

---

Restore Vitality — to live more fully. Bragg

explorers of the American continent found the natives to be wonderful physical specimens. The tragic sequence many be seen in the deterioration of the remaining American Indians today, whose health and lives have been destroyed by the white man's salt, alcohol and devitalized foods . . . in far greater numbers than those who were killed in the early days of our history by the white man's guns.

I have made many expeditions to the far primitive corners of the earth, and I have never found the natives salt users. None of them suffered from high blood pressure . . . in fact, regardless of age, they generally had the perfect blood pressure of 120/80. They suffered from no kidney or heart diseases. Their diets varied, but all ate the foods natural to their particular environment . . . and all used no salt.

In fact, this is the same sort of situation I discovered among the wonderful people of Southeastern Europe on my very first research expedition after leaving Dr. Rollier's Sanatorium. These people ate natural foods, which were cultivated in their own gardens. Some of the vegetables, like the cabbage which thrived there, had been originally introduced from other lands . . . but over generations had become native foods. As mentioned before, their diet was rich in lactic acid . . . and completely salt-free . . . the main staple being that delicious salt-free sauerkraut.

THE HISTORY OF SAUERKRAUT

It has been said that a sure way of getting oneself murdered in Germany is to question whether sauerkraut is "a dish for the gods." Certainly sauerkraut (unfortunately, usually made with salt) is a star of German cuisine; and cabbage farming and sauerkraut manufacture are important factors in that country's economy.

But this "national dish of the Germans" actually had its origin thousands of miles to the east and centuries before Germany became a country. The ancient Romans brought the recipe from China, as we mentioned earlier. Whether they also brought back the native Chinese cabbage, which is similar to Cos lettuce . . . or whether they developed a cultivated variety from the wild, scrawny leafed cabbage native to the chalk cliffs of England

23

. . . is not clear. However, the cultivation of headed cabbage is recorded by the Roman historian Pliny, who also described the technique of adding salt to shredded cabbage and allowing it to ferment to make a delicacy served at Roman feasts.

After the fall of Rome, the Oriental-Roman cabbage recipe was apparently forgotten in Europe until the 13th century, when the conquering Tatar hordes reintroduced it from China into Austria. It was the Austrians who gave the modern dish its name — literally, "sauer" meaning sour, and "Kraut" meaning greens or plant. They passed it along to their neighbors, and sauerkraut was welcomed and taken to the hearts — or stomachs — of the Germans. Its fame spread throughout Europe and into the British Isles, where the famous Captain Cook atributed the health of his crew in great part to the large quantities of sauerkraut fed to them. It was generally considered that sauerkraut was more easily digestible than ordinary cabbage.

Bailey's "Cyclopedia of Horticulture" credits the scrawny wild cabbage of the English Channel cliffs as the ancestor of most European varieties of cabbage. Its cultivation as a food staple developed from the plant's capacity for using the more abundant food supply furnished by cultivation, and storing it in a way to make it available for man's use. The "gigantic bud" or "head" of closely packed leaves, developed especially by the Germans for making sauerkraut, is formed during a prolonged second part of the plant's early stage of rapid leaf-and-plant growth. For edibility and marketability, the cabbage must be picked at this stage before it starts blooming and going to seed.

This type of cabbage thrives best in a moist and comparatively cool climate. It is sensitive to both over-heating and freezing, and needs sunlight, moisture and aerated soil.

MEDICINAL QUALITIES OF CABBAGE

It is interesting to note that many herbs and plants whose medicinal qualities were known and used, although not chemically analyzed, by the ancients are now being utilized in modern medicine.

Cabbage was among those favored by the Greeks and Romans as medicine. Now it is being rediscovered as an important source of antibiotics.

24

As defined by the U.S. Government "Yearbook of Agriculture", an antibiotic is an organic chemical substance produced by a plant, an animal or a micro-organism, which selectively checks the growth of bacteria, viruses, fungi and other disease-producing organisms or completely destroys them. Since 1943, research has been progressively successful in discovering the natural antibiotic activities of green plants.

At the New York State Agricultural Experiment Station, C.S. Pedersen and Paul Fisher discovered that the undesirable gram-negative aerobic bacteria on the surface of cabbage leaves ordinarily disappear shortly after the cabbage is cut. These scientists attribute this antibiotic action to the presence of a bacteriacidal substance in the cabbage tissue, which causes reduction or destruction of the dangerous bacteria within 6 to 24 hours. They also noted that this beneficial substance is inactivated by heat.

THE BACTERIOLOGY OF SAUERKRAUT

In reporting on the bacteriology of sauerkraut in "The Chemistry and Technology of Food and Food Products, Vol. II", Morris B. Jacobs also notes the presence of gram-negative, low-acid or nonacid producing organisms which were on the cabbage when cut, which were discovered in the freshly packed vat for making sauerkraut. He attributes the disappearance of these undesirable organisms to environmental factors such as the herbs concentration and lack of oxygen.

A second group of organisms then appear, consisting of gas-producing cocci, whose predominant species produces lactic and acetic acids, alcohol and carbon dioxide from glucose, and mannitol from fructose. These initiate the kraut fermentation, reaching a peak between the first and second days during which the acidity reaches from 0.7 to 0.9% (at lower temperatures, 0.8 to 1.0%). Best temperature for growth is 77 degrees Fahrenheit. This group adds to the pleasant flavor of the sauerkraut.

As the second group gradually dies off after the second day, a third group, the lactobacilli, start to multiply rapidly and reach a maximum between the third and fifth days of fermentation. The principal member of this group is a non-gas producing organism which ferments the natural sugars chiefly into lactic acid without production of gas. Under ideal conditions it can increase the acidity as high as 1.5%.

After the fifth day, this third group gradually disappears, and the fermentation of the sauerkraut is completed by a fourth group of bacteria, which reach a peak at the end of seven days. Capable of producing as high as 2.4% acid, this group causes fermentation whose principal products are lactic and acetic acids, alcohol, and carbon dioxide from glucose, mannitol from fructose.

Bacteriologist Jacobs advises that the best way to make good sauerkraut is to control such factors as the herbs, temperature, kind and quality of cabbage, cleanliness of the vats, and general sanitation. If these factors are controlled satisfactorily, he notes, the shredded cabbage will undergo a normal fermentation in which there will be a natural sequence of bacterial populations, each of which will contribute its share to the flavor and natural chemical composition of the finished sauerkraut.

NUTRIENTS IN SAUERKRAUT

The "Yearbook of Agriculture" analyzes the nutrients in one cup of sauerkraut as follows: Water, 91%; calories, 30; protein, 2 grams; fat, trace; carbohydrates, 7 grams; calcium, 54 milligrams; iron, 0.8 milligrams; Vitamin A, 60 I.U.; thiamose, .05 milligrams; riboflavin, .1 milligrams; niacin, .2 milligrams; ascorbic acid, 24 milligrams.

SALT IS NOT NECESSARY TO MAKE
DELICIOUS AND NUTRITIOUS SAUERKRAUT

Who would want to kill the effect of these nutrients with salt? Yet there are many people who have the preconceived idea that salt is neccessary in the making of sauerkraut.

This is not true! It is not the salt — but the pulverized ground dill, celery and caraway seeds and the water, plus the cabbage itself, which cause the fermentation.

If you have been living on a salt-free diet, as I do, the salt-free sauerkraut will have a delicious, satisfying and refreshing taste.

Others, who have been accustomed to eating heavily salted foods (including salted sauerkraut), are likely to complain that anything salt-free "has no taste" or "tastes flat." You may suggest that they use kelp seasoning as a substitute. But if they insist on putting poison on their food, let them add the salt!

It is, of course, impossible today to purchase salt-free sauerkraut in supermarkets. Not only are the popular supermarket brands heavily loaded with salt, but they also contain the powerful chemical preservative benzoate of soda. In my opinion, this chemical is harmful to the body chemistry and should not enter the human body.

HOME-MADE SALT-FREE SAUERKRAUT IS A TASTE DELIGHT

In order to get full advantage of the great health and nutritional qualities of salt-free sauerkraut . . . as well as its most delicious flavors . . . you are forced to make it in your own kitchen. And let me tell you that this is very easy . . . and the more you do it, the easier it becomes. Home-made salt-free sauerkraut is so delicious, so far superior to any commercial brand, that you will consider it well worth the effort ten times over!

Just think . . . from the day you start to make it, in seven days you will have not only a wonderfully delicious dish of natural food . . . but you will have one that also contains abundant amounts of health-building lactic acid.

You can make salt-free sauerkraut with cabbage alone . . . or you can make it a variety of ways as we do in the Bragg kitchen, adding onions, garlic, sliced carrots and celery. There is always a jar of salt-free sauerkraut in our refrigerator. Many guests from all over the world come to our home for health meals . . . and we have not yet found one person who did not ask for the second dish of our specialty, salt-free sauerkraut! They love it as we do . . . they revel in eating it.

I LEARNED TO MAKE SALT-FREE SAUERKRAUT FROM TWO EXPERTS — BOTH OVER 100 YEARS OLD

Again we go back to my first expedition in my long career of health and nutritional research, more than seventy years ago.

For more than a year, I carried on my research work on the health and long life of the people in Southeast Europe. My journal was filled with notes about the many youthful, vigorous, long-lived people whom I had met, talked with and eaten with.

I had accumulated all the information I needed to convince me that lactic acid was a master health food. Having eaten it for more than a year, I never felt or was stronger in my life.

Now I told my guide Andrei that I wanted to learn from an expert how to make that wonderful salt-free sauerkraut. Andrei replied that the people who would teach me were a husband and wife, both more than 100 years of age.

It was a three-day hike to their home, far into the rugged mountain country. But we made it joyfully, as we found perfect paradise far away from civilization.

The home of this couple lay in a beautiful valley with great, towering mountains on both sides. The heavy snows of winter brought new top soil to their farm every year. When we arrived, everything was so green! There before our eyes was one of the most magnificent organic gardens I ever saw. No wonder this man and wife were still enjoying life after one hundred years on this earth!

When I met them I could hardly believe my eyes . . . they looked not more than sixty years of age. No glasses, no hearing aids, no stiffness of body. Both had bright, healthy, clear eyes with not a broken vein in them . . . like the eyes of young, healthy children. There was a glow to their skin . . . skin and muscle tone were those of persons one-fourth their age.

They greeted me as if I were a long-lost friend. Andrei explained that I wanted to learn how to make salt-free sauerkraut from experts. They just smiled . . . they were both very modest people.

They showed us their organic garden and told us how they believed in the cycle of life . . . they believed that everything must return to the compost pile. Theirs was composed of top soil, manure, leaves, and all kinds of organic vegetation so rich in nutrients.

Many people go through life committing partial suicide — destroying their health, youth, talents, energies and creative qualities. Indeed, to learn how to be good to oneself is often more difficult than to learn how to be good to others.
—Joshua Liebman

The unexamined life is not worth living. It is time to re-evaluate your past as a guide to your future.
—Socrates

Then they showed us the cabbage patch. What firm, luscious cabbage! You could smell its pungent, refreshing odor. They showed us their garlic, explaining to Andrei how important it was in their diet. Then the other vegetables . . . the carrots were a dark, rich yellow, the onions firm, the celery a bright green.

These were the ingredients . . . this was the setting . . . these were the experts who taught me the secret of making salt-free sauerkraut . . . the Balkan way.

Let me share it with you . . . including some flavorful, healthful and helpful adaptations developed over the decades of experience in making this delicious, nutritious salt-free sauerkraut in the Bragg kitchen.

"Now learn what and how great benefits a temporate diet will bring along with it. In the first place you will enjoy good health." —Horace

---

"Wisdom does not show itself so much in precept as in life — a firmness of mind and mastery of appetite." —Seneca

---

UNCOMPLICATE YOUR LIVING

Living is a continual lesson in problem solving, but the trick is to know where to start. No excuses — start your Health Program Today.

THE BRAGG-BALKAN METHOD OF MAKING SALT-FREE SAUERKRAUT

INGREDIENTS

1. **Cabbage** ... the greener, the better.

Sauerkraut can be made with shredded cabbage alone ... after all, that is what sauerkraut is! But the people of the Balkans make their salt-free sauerkraut with the addition of other raw vegetables, which ferment along with the cabbage and add richness both to the nutritious lactic acid content and the delicious flavor.

2. **Other Raw Vegetables** ... optional but recommended for variety.

SLICED: Onions, Carrots, Turnips
WHOLE: Small green tomatoes, Small Cucumbers, Small Red Peppers
CHOPPED: Garlic, Celery, Cauliflower

Prepare vegetables ... and keep in separate piles until you pack the sauerkraut. Proportion these vegetables to the sauerkraut (packing in layers — sauerkraut, vegetables, sauerkraut, etc.) ... as well as the selection of vegetables, spices to add ... depends upon your taste. In the Bragg kitchen, we enjoy both the plain and the combined sauerkraut with vegetables.

3. **Seed Spices** ... measured, then pulverized.

1½ HEAPING TABLESPOONS EACH of Caraway, Dill and Celery Seed, measured before pulverizing, PER AVERAGE HEAD OF CABBAGE.

"Health is ... a blessing that money cannot buy." —*Izaak Walton.*

The seeds may be used whole, but they release much more flavor when ground or pulverized. This may be done in an electric seed grinder or in the high speed blender . . . or you may use a rolling pin, or the real old-fashioned method of pestle and mortar. You may mix the seeds together before packing the sauerkraut, but keep this "spice mixute" separate from other ingredients until packing.

The proportion of seeds to cabbage given above is the minimum . . . it is all right to use a little more. Again, your taste and judgment are the criterion.

It is this seed-spice mixture which aids the fermentation and helps produce the lactic acid.

4. Bragg Special Additions . . . optional but recommended.

When making salt-free sauerkraut in the Bragg kitchen, we have added these ingredients to the Balkan recipe:

To the Seed-Spice Mixture: 1 tablespoon each of KELP SEASONING and GARLIC POWDER, per head of cabbage. Kelp adds iodine and many nutrients from the sea to your mixture.

To RAW Vegetables: The proportion of GARLIC which we use is 2 heaping tablespoons or 6 garlic cloves, minced, per head of cabbage. We mix some of this in every layer when "packing."

UTENSILS:

WARNING: Do not use aluminum utensils of any kind in making this salt-free sauerkraut (or at any time, for that matter!). This includes knives, spoons, pans, etc., used in preparing the ingredients. The aluminum migrates at double speed from utensil to food in a lactic acid climate, causing a chemical reaction that is definitely harmful. Never let any aluminum touch any of the ingredients!

Use only stainless steel in the preparation of your ingredients.

For making the sauerkraut, an earthen crock is the best type

"Our prayers should be for a sound mind in a healthy body." —*Juvenal.*

"Govern well thy appetite, lest Sin surprise thee, and her black attendant Death."
—*Milton.*

of utensil. Then the second choice, a large glass container (available free at restaurants as used mayonnaise, mustard jars, etc.) The usual size is a one-gallon crock or container. However, if you have a large family or entertain a great deal and want to make a larger quantity of salt-free sauerkraut for them, you may use a two-gallon or three-gallon size.

This crock or container is not to be covered in the conventional manner. When you pack the mixture (as described in "Directions") there will be a 3-inch space from the top of the mixture to the top of the container, to allow for bubbling while fermentation is in progress.

To hold the packed mixture in place during the fermenting process, you will need a round plate slightly smaller in diameter than the mouth of the container . . . and a well-scrubbed stone to use as a weight on top of the plate.

And, of course, be sure that all utensils are absolutely CLEAN and DRY.

DIRECTIONS:

Wash all vegetables thoroughly.

Shred the cabbage, using a stainless steel shredder (which you can purchase at any Health Food Store or in the household department of any large department store), or a sharp stainless steel knife.

Prepare other ingredients, as previously directed.

Pack shredded cabbage firmly across the bottom of the crock or glass container in a layer 1 to 1½ inches deep . . . then a smaller layer of onions (or one of the other raw vegetables) to complete a 2-inch layer across the bottom. Over this layer sprinkle some of the seed-spice mixture and chopped garlic. Mix the entire layer lightly with your fingertips, then pack firmly again.

Repeat . . . 2-inch layer by 2-inch layer of cabbage (mixing in seed-spice mixture) and another vegetable sprinkled with garlic and even the seed-spice mixture if you desire more spice flavor . . . until crock or container is filled within 3 inches of the top. Now cover the entire mixture with pure cold water. In the Bragg kitchen, we use only steam-processed distilled water . . . and I recommend distilled water for the best tasting salt-free sauerkraut.

Retain some of the larger outer cabbage leaves when preparing cabbage for final cover of sauerkraut. This protects the upper most layer from oxidization while fermenting. Cover outer leaves with clean muslin or cloth working down along the sides of the jar.

Place the plate-cover on top of the cloth, pressing it firmly so that the liquid flows over it. Put the scrubbed stone on top of the plate to hold it in place.

Cover the container with a clean dish towel and set it in a warm room to work. The temperature should be maintained between 70° and 80°F . . . otherwise, the fermentation will not take place and the cabbage will go soft. If the sauerkraut mixture has not started "working" or bubbling within 48 hours, the temperature of your storage area is too low . . . Place a lighted light bulb near the container and cover the whole thing with canvas or an old blanket to help maintain the correct temperature.

Warning: Your sauerkraut may really ferment in a big way, and overflow the crock. If this happens, place the container in a glass pie plate to catch the juices. **Do not use a metal overflow vessel** . . . keep all metal away from your sauerkraut!

FERMENTATION PERIOD

Be sure to watch your sauerkraut during the fermentation process . . . checking it several times daily. Train your nose to smell the degree of fermentation from day to day.

Skim off any scum that appears on the surface . . . and make absolutely sure that the plate and scrubbed stone are keeping the mixture completely submerged under the fermenting liquid. Remove muslin, plate and stone when needed and rinse thoroughly and replace.

The average time required to complete the fermentation process is 7 days . . . but it may require 8 or 9 or even 10 days, depending upon the temperature maintained.

Taste your sauerkraut on the 7th day . . . it should have that traditional fermented taste. If not, let it ferment a day or two more, until it "tastes right."

Remove from crock and pack into fruit jars and cap. Then . . . into your refrigerator it goes . . . ready for serving as a special dish by itself . . . or in a wide variety of delightful combinations, cold or warm. Sauerkraut may be stored in a covered crock in cool area and servings taken as needed. Maintain moisture level to top of sauerkraut keeping muslin plate and stone clean.

NOTE: If you prefer to make your salt-free sauerkraut with cabbage only, or combined with only a few vegetables, the same directions apply . . . a 2-inch layer sprinkled with seed-spice mixture and packed firmly . . . repeat to within 3 inches of top.

SALT-FREE SAUERKRAUT AS THE FIRST COURSE

At the Bragg home when we eat salt-free sauerkraut it is among the first courses. It may be served alone or in various combinations.

Our favorite method is to use our salt-free sauerkraut as a topping to our regular salad. The standard Bragg salad is called "Nature's Broom," because it really gives the intestines bulk, moisture and lubrication. Remember, constipation is one of the basic causes of autointoxication or self-poisoning . . . and a generous amount of coarse raw vegetables plus salt-free sauerkraut greatly aid in defeating this vicious condition. In my opinion, one bowel movement per day is not sufficient to clean the rectum of fecal matter. Out-go should equal intake . . . in other words, you should have a bowel movement upon arising and within several hours after eating each meal. The bulk provided in the Bragg "New Broom" salad topped with salt-free sauerkraut is important in helping to establish regularity of the bowels.

Our "New Broom" salad is composed of raw grated carrots, raw grated beets, chopped raw cabbage and chopped raw celery. To these basic ingredients, you may add any other raw vegetables you wish . . . such as lettuce, watercress, endive, parsley and over the top sliced avocado and tomato.

Top this salad with a generous helping of salt-free sauerkraut. This makes the most perfect delicious first course you can find for a real health meal.

USE YOUR IMAGINATION
IN SERVING SALT-FREE SAUERKRAUT

There are many delightful and tasty ways to serve salt-free sauerkraut. Another Bragg favorite is to serve this dish with the addition of natural cider vinegar ... this gives it a delicious and zesty flavor.

Other tasty additions to salt-free sauerkraut as a cold dish include sliced tomatoes, garlic, onions, parsley, apples. Some people like to add sesame seeds or sunflower seeds.

As a warm dish, at the Bragg home we like to combine salt-free sauerkraut with such vegetables as squash, tomatoes, onions, celery, carrots, beets. Sometimes we combine it with red cabbage, which gives an appetizing color contrast and a refreshing medley of different textures.

All you have to do is to use your imagination in preparing salt-free sauerkraut dishes ... and you will come up with some interesting and tasty results. But also ... don't forget that good, plain, salt-free sauerkraut just as it comes from the crock is very delicious ... and nutritious!

DON'T OVER-HEAT SALT-FREE SAUERKRAUT

We must always remember that in eating salt-free sauerkraut, we are getting an abundant supply of lactic acid and precious, wonder-working enzymes. That is why you obtain the greatest nutritional value when you eat it cold and uncooked.

However, you can retain many nutrients if you **remember to use low heat in preparing cooked salt-free sauerkraut dishes.** Over-heating, of course, will destroy the valuable lactic acid and enzymes ... so watch that cooking temperature!

Nature never deceives us; it is always we who deceive ourselves. *Rousseau*

Every man is the builder of a Temple, called his body. *Henry David Thoreau*

Good health and good sense are two of life's greatest blessings.
Maxim 827 Pubilius Syrus

SALT-FREE SAUERKRAUT DISHES FROM AROUND THE WORLD

People all over the world eat sauerkraut . . . and each country or area has its own special dishes. We have selected some choice recipes to include in this book . . . first, from Southeastern Europe, where I first learned to make salt-free sauerkraut . . . then from other countries, whose recipes we have adapted from salty to salt-free sauerkraut.

I want you to enjoy these recipes from around the world. They can appeal to both vegetarians and conventional meat eaters. I am sure you all are aware that through the hundreds of years you can find both meat eaters and vegetarian groups. This is the reason for some of both — but for the vegetarians each one of the meat recipes can have delicious substitutes like brown rice, beans, soya beans, etc. Soya bean mash (you make this yourself — cook, mash; then add olive oil, chopped garlic, kelp, and herbs to taste) is a delicious spread for the Krautwiches. You can do this also with any of the beans — even lentils and garbanzos. I usually soak these the night before cooking to make the cooking time shorter. Even lima beans make a delicious krautwich spread. Also these spreads are delicious added as a topping on the Sauerkraut salads.

VEGETARIAN AND MEAT DIETS FOUND AROUND THE WORLD

I have been both in my life-time — a vegetarian and a meat eater. But the more I see of customs around the world, I feel it is almost a personal habit one falls into early in life. I became a vegetarian when I arrived in Switzerland in search of my health I had lost with devitalized foods. I want each one of you reading this Sauerkraut book to work out your diet what does the best for you — for your energy and health! You be the master of your bodily needs. If you keep a chart of your energy ups and downs, it will amaze you how they differ with what you eat! Of course your thinking is important also. I think health, youth and energy at all times and feel around 21 most of the time. Yes — does this amaze you — it does even my daughter Patricia for I can outdo most of her young friends when it comes to hiking, dancing and energy outgo.

36

I want you healthy and happy and I know mealtime is important — so may this little book help put spice into your mealtime and add a glow of health and energy to your daily living.

Life at the longest goes too fast. I can remember when I was a boy of five — like it was yesterday — where does time go — so dear friend, use it wisely and take good care of your physical home with wise meal planning. I want you to know health living can be so thrilling and please use wisdom and follow the right road to radiant health.

Here are the recipes for you to try in your own kitchen . . . and remember, keep the heat low when cooking!

You might want to note, next to a recipe you tried, the addition of special seasonings your family prefers, the preparation time, a special way to serve the dish, or menu ideas that you have found especially successful.

We are leaving some blank pages for your favorite family health sauerkraut recipes that you may develop.

I hope you will share any new Sauerkraut recipes with us.

Keep Healthy and Happy,

Paul C. Bragg

If mankind would at once discard all refined, sprayed, and unnatural foods, it would be the beginning of a race of people that would live long happy lives and be free of disease.
—*Paul C. Bragg*

Many people go throughout life committing partial suicide — destroying their health, youth, beauty, talents, energies, creative qualities. Indeed, to learn how to be good to oneself is often more difficult than to learn how to be good to others.
—*Paul C. Bragg*

Be proud you live a natural health life. —*Patricia Bragg*

S·O·O·O FLAVORFUL

Delicious Healthful Sauerkraut Recipes

Now that you have a crock of savory sauerkraut, you can bring it to the table in various appetizing guises. Try adding a teaspoon of caraway seeds to a cup of sauerkraut. Serve it cold or hot but don't subject it to prolonged heating. This kills the valuable enzymes in the raw cabbage.

Try adding diced unpeeled (if unsprayed) apples to the sauerkraut. This, too, can be heated but serve it while the apples are still crisp. It is most delicious.

Try heating some sauerkraut with another raw vegetable — chopped celery, grated carrot or even shredded fresh cabbage. Red cabbage provides a nice color contrast and an interesting medley of textures.

Of course sauerkraut fresh from fermentation, without salt and without preservatives is a marvelous accompaniment to any meal.

Don't overlook the possible uses for that mineral rich juice which is also a fountain of lactic acid ferment.

If you have been cutting salt out of your diet, you will find the flavor of saltless sauerkraut refreshing, and satisfying. Some members of your family who haven't yet learned how to live without the salt shaker may find the flavor a little flat. Let them add various herbs and seasonings to taste or more kelp.

The surprising thing about salt-free sauerkraut is that the salt is not necessary to the fermentation process.

Salt-Free Sauerkraut

FOR GOOD HEALTH!

SALADS WITH ZINGY HEALTHY KRAUT FLAVOR

BRAGG "NEW BROOM" LACTOBACILLIUS HEALTH SALAD

1 juice orange
1 carrot grated
1 beet grated
1 c celery chopped
1 c cabbage chopped
1 c purple cabbage chopped
1 green bell pepper diced
½ red bell pepper diced
1 cucumber diced
3 tomatoes diced
  chopped endive
  chives
  Chinese parsley

1 avocado sliced
1 head lettuce — butter or
  bronze
  Health Mayonnaise
3 green onions chopped
½ c Jerusalem artichoke
  chopped
2 tbsp pine nuts
½ c alfalfa sprouts
⅓ c fresh green peas
2 c Health Sauerkraut
  celery tops
  chopped parsley

Spices to taste; salad herbs, dill seed, olive or unsaturated oil, cider vinegar, garlic powder, kelp seasoning. Grate beet, carrot, chop all ingredients fine and combine. Squeeze juice of orange over and mix — place in refrigerator till serving. When serving add layer of sauerkraut, tomatoes and avocado.

Bragg Salad Dressing: Mix dressing ingredients and pour over salad prior to serving, add health mayonnaise, and if desired, Roquefort or goat cheese crumbs to taste. *Serves 4 to 6.*

"ZOURKOOL" POTATO SALAD DRESSING
Dutch

½ c sauerkraut juice
½ c homemade mayonnaise

½ tsp kelp seasoning
garlic, herbs to season

Try a sauerkraut dressing on your potato salad. Combine sauerkraut juice with homemade mayonnaise, seasonings, garlic and kelp. Beat until smooth and refrigerate. When dinner is about ready, pour the dressing over the potato salad and toss gently. Garnish with snipped parsley and watercress.

PINEAPPLE SAUERKRAUT

2 lbs fresh sauerkraut
5 c unsweetened pineapple juice
1½ to 2-lb ripe pineapple

Drain sauerkraut. Wash thoroughly under running water, and let soak in pot of cold water 10 to 20 minutes. Squeeze a handful at a time until completely dry.

Combine sauerkraut and pineapple juice in heavy 3-4 pint saucepan. Bring to a boil, stirring and separating sauerkraut strands with fork. Reduce to lowest heat, cover tightly, and simmer 1½ to 2 hours (until sauerkraut has absorbed most of the liquid).

Cut the top 1½" from the pineapple and set aside. Hollow the pineapple carefully, leaving ⅛" to ¼" of fruit in the shell. Discard the woody core. Cut fruit into ¼" cubes.

Stir diced pineapple into cooked sauerkraut, and cook 1 or 2 minutes. Pour mixture into large sieve over bowl. When drained, pour sauerkraut-fruit mixture into pineapple shell. Cover with pineapple top and serve.

Note: In Germany, this is traditionally served with roasted game birds.

HAWAIIAN PINEAPPLE-SAUERKRAUT SALAD

2 c drained sauerkraut
½ c sour cream
¼ c honey
½ c chopped toasted pecans
* or almonds*

1 can (20 oz) or fresh
* pineapple tidbits, drained*
¼ c golden seedless raisins
* (sultanas)*
lettuce

Toss together kraut, pineapple, sour cream, honey and raisins. Chill several hours or overnight.

Before serving, mix in nuts, reserving some for garnish. Turn salad into lettuce-lined bowl. Sprinkle with nuts. *Makes 1 qt*

STEP LIVELY ASPIC

An aspic chock-full of diced fresh vegetables is a splendid, refreshing salad anytime. Make it with kraut juice for that extra special zip.

3 c tomato juice
1 small sliced onion
1 small bay leaf
   seasonings to taste
1 c sauerkraut juice
½ c each: diced carrot,
   celery, green pepper

1 stalk celery
2 slices lemon
1 tsp kelp seasoning
2 envelopes unflavored
   gelatin
   salad greens

Combine tomato juice, celery, onion, lemon, bay leaf, seasonings. Simmer, uncovered, 10 minutes. Strain.

Meanwhile sprinkle gelatin over kraut juice to soften; stir in hot mixture until gelatin is dissolved. Chill mixture until consistency of unbeaten egg white; then fold in vegetables. Pour into individual molds or 1-qt mold. Chill until firm. To serve: unmold onto salad greens. Serve with mayonnaise or sour cream. *Serve 6 to 8.*

GREEN COLE SLAW AND SAUERKRAUT

2 c crisp shredded cabbage
1 c salt-free sauerkraut
½ c chopped parsley
⅓ c green onions, sliced thin

1 tbsp honey
1 tbsp apple cider vinegar
2 tbsp unsaturated oil or
   mayonnaise
kelp, mixed herbs, garlic to taste

Prepare cabbage, parsley and green onions; combine. Mix honey, vinegar, oil or mayonnaise and mix with salad and chill til served. Optional — add chopped watercress, chopped celery, grated raw beet, or grated raw carrot. You can make up different combinations each time til you find your favorite.

ZESTY, TANGY
SAUERKRAUT SOUPS

SAUERKRAUT SOUP HUNGARIAN

1 *lb salt-free sauerkraut*
1 *chopped onion*
2 *oz whole wheat flour*
   kelp seasoning

1 *c stock*
1 *oz safflower oil*
1 *tsp paprika*
½ *pint sour cream*

Simmer sauerkraut with 2 pints water and stock for 30 minutes.
Saute onions in oil until transparent. Stir in flour and cook for
1 minute. Add paprika and seasoning, mix well with flour. Pour
in stock from sauerkraut stirring all the time. Add sauerkraut.
Simmer for 10 minutes.

SKABU KAPOSTU SUPA

from Latvia
(Sauerkraut Soup for Conventional Meat Eaters)
Vegetarians can use lentils, brown rice, etc. as substitutes.

1½ *lbs meat brisket*
  3 *qts water*
  1 *large chopped onion*
  2 *c (1 lb) chopped salt-free*
    sauerkraut

¼ *c (2½ oz) barley*
½ *tsp kelp seasoning*
¼ *c sour cream*
2 *sliced tomatoes*
2 *peeled, cored and sliced*
  apples

Bring the meat and cold water to a boil, then drain off water
and add the same amount again. Bring to a boil and add onion,
sauerkraut, and washed barley and cook for about 2 hours; add
kelp seasoning, as needed, and sour cream. If desired, sliced
tomatoes and apples may also be added, and cooked during the
last ½ hour before serving. The sour cream or barley may be
left out. Instead of meat — meat substitutes may be used; in
that case, add a little more kelp seasoning. *Serves 6.*

SHAKE-A-LEG CHICKEN WITH COOL KRAUT

5 c salt-free sauerkraut	2 chopped medium green
1 jar (4 oz) drained and	peppers
chopped pimiento	2 chopped medium onions
¼ tsp paprika	misc herbs, garlic to taste
kelp seasoning	½ c butter or safflower oil
¼ c cider vinegar	½ c honey
2 tbsp arrowroot	¼ c water
12 chicken legs with thighs	

Drain kraut, reserving liquid. Toss kraut with green pepper, pimiento, half the onion, paprika and kelp to taste. Chill until serving time.

Saute remaining onion and the garlic in butter until golden. Add vinegar, honey, kelp to taste and kraut liquid. Stir until honey dissolves; bring to a boil over medium heat. Blend arrowroot with water and stir into sauce mixture. Continue boiling for 1 minute, stirring constantly. Remove from heat.

Place chicken on grill 7 to 8 inches from source of heat; cook 10 minutes. Brush with sauce and grill 10 minutes longer. Turn chicken and grill 10 minutes, or until done, brushing frequently with sauce to glaze. Serve with kraut relish. *Serves 8.*

ZINGY BARBECUE SAUCE

⅓ c minced onion	¼ c unsaturated oil
1½ c chili sauce	3 tbsp honey or raw sugar
1 tsp mustard powder	2 tbsp amino acids
garlic, kelp to taste	½ c sauerkraut juice

In small saucepan, saute onion in oil until tender, but not brown. Stir in remaining ingredients and simmer 10 minutes. Serve over meats. *Makes about 2 cups.*

BAR·B·CUE

TOMATOKRAUT

½ c sliced onions
2 tbsp unsaturated oil
1 tbsp soy or wheat flour
4 c salt-free sauerkraut
1½ c tomato juice
2 bay leaves
garlic, herbs and kelp seasoning to taste

For an appetizing change try tomato sauerkraut. Saute half cup of sliced onions in two tablespoons of oil just until golden. Add flour, sauerkraut, tomato juice, 2 bay leaves and 1 teaspoon of kelp. Simmer at low heat for about 15 minutes. Remove the bay leaves and stir in one tablespoon of raw honey. *Serves 4.*

SAUERKRAUT — GERMAN

2 lb salt-free sauerkraut
1 chopped onion
10 juniper berries
1 grated potato
4 oz salt-free butter
¾ pint stock
kelp, garlic, misc herbs to taste

Lightly brown onion in butter. Add sauerkraut and juniper berries. Pour in a stock, simmer for ½ hour. Add potato 15 minutes before serving.

GOULASH WITH SAUERKRAUT
GERMAN

2 lb veal
2 oz safflower oil
2 onions
8 oz tomatoes
½ pint sour cream
¼ tsp paprika
2 c salt-free sauerkraut
kelp, garlic, misc herbs to taste

Cut the veal into 1-inch squares. Slice onion and brown in safflower oil. Add meat and brown on all sides. Add the peeled quartered tomatoes, season with kelp seasoning, garlic and paprika. Cover with water and lid and simmer for 1½ hours. Strain sauce, simmer meat lightly to reduce it. Add cream and simmer for 3-4 minutes. Pour sauce over meat, re-heat and serve with salt-free sauerkraut.

SAUERKRAUT STUFFED PEPPER
SPANISH

3 medium green peppers   ½ c dry wholewheat bread
½ c salt-free sauerkraut   crumbs
1 thin slice onion   ½ tsp paprika
              kelp, garlic, misc herbs to taste

Cut piece off stem of each pepper and remove the seeds and
partitions then par boil in boiling water for 5 minutes. Mix
remaining ingredients and fill peppers. Place in oiled dish, top
with wholewheat bread crumbs and pour ½ inch water or stock
into pan. Bake in a moderate oven for 30 minutes. Serve hot.
Serves 3.

SAUERKRAUT WITH APRICOTS

2½ lb salt-free sauerkraut   1½ tsp poppy seed
  ½ c stock   2 tbsp honey
  2 tbsp salt-free butter or   1 c diced dry apricots
  safflower oil

Combine all ingredients except sauerkraut in large skillet. Simmer for 30-40 minutes, last 5 minutes add sauerkraut. Serve hot.

BIGOS
Sauerkraut Stew, Polish Style

1½ lb salt-free sauerkraut
  1 sliced onion
  1 oz soya flour
  1 oz salt-free butter
    kelp seasoning
  1 lb cooked meat or poultry
    (not Mutton)
  1 pint stock
    paprika, herbs to taste

Simmer sauerkraut in the stock for ½ hour. Saute the onion in
1 oz butter, add the soya flour and cook for 1 minute. Chop
sauerkraut and add onion mixture to it. Cut meat into small
pieces. Put meat and sauerkraut mixture into casserole, season
with kelp, herbs and mix well. Cook in slow oven, covered, for
1 hour.

REBHUHNER mit SAUERKRAUT
(Partridges with Sauerkraut)

3 large young partridges
1 tsp kelp seasoning
misc herbs, garlic to taste
3 tbsp salt-free butter
1 crushed juniper berry
3 medium-sized carrots,
quartered
water, if needed

2 tbsp hot water, or more
1 to 2 tsp flour, if needed
1 tbsp cold water, if needed
½ c sour cream
1½ lbs salt-free sauerkraut
2 tbsp salt-free butter
6 small white onions or
shallots

Clean partridges. Rub kelp seasoning and herbs inside each bird and on backs. Melt butter in heavy iron pan and saute partridges in the butter, turning them until the birds are brown on all sides. Put in the crushed juniper berry, the carrots, and the small onions. Cover pot and simmer very slowly until partridges are tender. Baste with hot water sparingly from time to time. To make sauce for the partridges; strain gravy. Mix whole wheat flour with cold water to a smooth paste, add to the gravy in the pan, and fold in the sour cream. Season with kelp, garlic and herbs, allow to come to a boil and thicken. Cut partridges in half and arrange on hot platter. Serve gravy in sauce boat. The sauerkraut is cooked by putting it into a saucepan with the butter, a little water may be added if needed. Cover pot and allow sauerkraut to cook slowly for ½ hour, until it is tender and the liquid is reduced. Serve this in a covered dish. Mashed or boiled (unpeeled) potatoes are served with this. *Serves 6.*

PATRICIA'S KRAUT CASSEROLE

½ c unsaturated oil
1 c chopped celery
1 c chopped onions
1 c grated carrots
1 c chopped bell pepper

1 tsp kelp seasoning
misc herbs, garlic to taste
4 c salt-free sauerkraut
Parmesan cheese
½ c diced pimentos

Saute all ingredients except kraut in oil until ½ cooked. Mix ½ ingredients with kraut and place in baking dish. Cover mixture with remainder of sauce. Cover with sliced tomatoes and sprinkle on Parmesan cheese. Bake in open casserole 25 minutes in pre-heated 250 degree oven. *Serves 6.*

MAN CAN LIVE BY . . . KRAUT RYE BREAD ALONE

What could be more tempting than bread baked at home? This rye bread has a slight tang that makes especially wonderful sandwiches.

1¼ c boiling water
kelp seasoning
1 package active dry yeast
½ c warm water (105⁰-115⁰)
3½ c sifted wholewheat flour
1 egg, slightly beaten

1 tbsp honey
2 tbsp butter or safflower oil
4 c sifted fine rye flour
2 c drained salt-free sauerkraut, chopped and
drained again

Combine boiling water, honey and kelp seasoning, and oil in large bowl; stir until butter melts. Sprinkle yeast over warm water; stir to dissolve. Stir into butter mixture. Add rye flour; beat smooth. Mix in 3½ cups whole wheat flour and the kraut. Turn dough onto floured board and knead 10 minutes or until smooth and elastic. Place in greased bowl; turn dough to grease all sides. Cover; let rise in warm place until doubled in bulk, about 45 minutes. Punch down; divide dough in half. Shape into 2 loaves; place in greased 9 x 5 x 3-inch loaf pans. Cover; let rise about 50 minutes. Brush with egg. Bake in 400⁰ (hot) oven 30 to 35 minutes. Cool on racks. *Makes 2 loaves.*

SAUERKRAUT WITH MUSHROOMS
RUSSIAN

1 lb salt-free sauerkraut   *1 oz dried mushrooms*
¼ pint sour cream

Cook mushrooms in small amount of water. Drain and reserve 4 tablespoons of the broth. Chop mushrooms and mix with sauerkraut. Add cream & broth — cook slowly for 20 minutes.

PECENA HUSA se ZELIM
CZECHOSLOVAKIAN
(Roast Goose with Sauerkraut)

1 goose — (10 to 12 lbs)
STUFFING:

1 tbsp unsaturated oil   *1 tsp kelp seasoning*
1 large minced onion   *misc herbs, garlic to taste*
2 lbs salt-free sauerkraut   *½ tsp poultry seasoning*
½ tsp caraway seeds,   *1 large potato (5 to 6 oz)*
*   optional*   *½ c pure water*

Clean and trim goose. Rub inside with kelp seasoning. Remove all fat from inside of goose and heat 1 tbsp. in pan. Saute onion in oil until light golden brown. Drain sauerkraut thoroughly. Add to onion. Add herbs, caraway seeds, etc. if desired. Allow to come to a boil. Grate potato into sauerkraut and cook until mixture thickens. Add water gradually if needed, being careful not to make the stuffing too moist. Stuff into goose, skewer or sew up opening.

Method of roasting: Roast goose in hot oven (450⁰F.) Prick skin all over and allow the fat to bake out before adding water. After 10 minutes, drain fat from roasting pan, turn goose, prick skin again and repeat. The skin will begin to brown. After draining off fat, pour in a little water at a time. It should be cold and poured over breast to make skin crisp. Baste with water every 8 or 10 minutes and keep turning goose till brown. The goose gravy is not thickened. Serve whole wheat flour dumplings with this, surrounding the goose with the dumplings. Keep these closely covered as they are only good if piping hot. The goose, in all Central European countries, is carved across the breast instead of lengthwise. The slices of breast are from 1 to 1½ in. wide. The skin of this roast goose should be brown and very crisp. *Serves 8.*

RINKEY-TINK KRAUT & APPLE SAUTE

Simple but superb with any casserole or poultry, a kraut and green apple saute.

3¼ c drained salt-free sauerkraut	3 c sliced pared green apples
2 tbsp red currant health jelly	¼ c honey or raw sugar
	¼ c butter or unsaturated oil

Combine kraut, apple, honey, jelly and seasonings. Place in oiled heavy skillet. Cook and stir kraut mixture over medium heat until lightly browned, about 15 minutes. Serve as relish. *Serves 6 to 8.*

I SCREAM YOU SCREAM FOR LEMONY KRAUT ICE CREAM

Kraut in ice cream? You're putting me on! The flavor is light, lemony and refreshing and the mixture delightfully creamy.

2 tbsp arrowroot	½ c honey or raw sugar
¼ c grated lemon peel (about 6 medium lemons)	1½ c milk
	2 eggs, separated
1 qt heavy whipped cream	½ c each: lemon juice, sauerkraut juice

Mix arrowroot, honey and lemon peel in saucepan; stir in milk. Cook over medium heat, stirring constantly, until mixture thickens and boils 1 minute. Remove from heat. Beat egg yolks in large bowl. Gradually blend in milk mixture. Cool. Stir in lemon juice and kraut juice. Beat egg whites until stiff, but not dry. Fold with cream into arrowroot mixture. Turn into refrigerator trays. Freeze until ice crystals form around edges of trays. Turn mixture into large bowl and beat well. Return to trays. Freeze until firm. Mellow in refrigerator for ½ hour before serving. *Makes 2 quarts.*

KRAUT ON THE HALF SHELL

Crunchy kraut and onion make the lowly baked potato a treat terrific.

8 medium baked potatoes	3 tbsp unsaturated oil
1 chopped onion	2½ c drained salt-free
Cheddar cheese, grated	sauerkraut
	paprika and kelp to taste

Bake potatoes in 375⁰ (moderate) oven 1 hour or until tender. Meanwhile, saute onion in oil about 2 minutes. Add kraut and cook 5 minutes longer. Cut slice off top of each potato. Scoop out remaining potato and mash, adding kraut mixture. Refill shells with potato mixture. Sprinkle grated cheese, paprika and kelp on top. Heat in 375⁰ oven about 10 minutes. *Serves 8.*

WHAT'S GOOD FOR THE GOOSE . . . IS KRAUT STUFFING

The goose that laid the golden egg makes mighty fine eating, roasted to a golden brown and brimming with piquant kraut stuffing. It wouldn't be a holiday without it.

1 large chopped onion	1 tbsp butter or soy oil
6½ c drained salt-free	1 medium apple, pared and
sauerkraut	diced
1½ c grated potatoes	1 small grated carrot
(2 medium)	2 tsp caraway seed
kelp, garlic to taste	poultry seasoning to taste
	11 to 12-pound goose

S·O·O·O FLAVORFUL

HUNGARIAN CABBAGE ROLLS
WITH SAUERKRAUT

1½ *lbs ground beef*
¼ *c uncooked brown rice*
2 *tbsp paprika*
1 *tsp kelp and herbs*
1 *c salt-free sauerkraut*
3 *lb head of cabbage*
1 *can whole tomatoes*
1 *clove garlic*
2 *large onions, thinly sliced*
1 *tsp unsaturated oil*
5 *tsp whole wheat flour*

Thoroughly mix ground beef, rice, 1 tbsp paprika, kelp & herbs to taste and juice from sauerkraut in bowl; let stand. In a 6-qt. kettle, steam 12 to 16 large outer leaves of cabbage in 1 c water, until limp. Remove leaves when limp; save water. Shred rest of cabbage; add to cabbage water together with onion, garlic, canned tomatoes, drained sauerkraut, 1 tbsp paprika. Cook over low heat until mixture is well heated and pot liquor covers mixture.

Make cabbage rolls by dividing meat mixture evenly between steamed leaves and folding leaves loosely and neatly. A toothpick may be used to secure roll but is not necessary. Place rolls on top of cooking mixture; cover and let simmer for two hours. Stir gently to keep the bottom from scorching.

Brown flour in oil. Drain some pot liquor to add to flour and oil for gravy. Add gravy to pot and stir enough to mix. Cook 10 min. Then it is ready to serve. *Serves 6.*

STUFFED CABBAGE ROLLS WITH SAUERKARUT IN TOMATO SAUCE

1 lb ground beef
1 small onion, chopped
1 egg
1 c cooked brown rice
½ c salt-free sauerkraut
½ tsp caraway seeds

1 tsp kelp
12 large cabbage leave,
    parboiled
2 cans (8 oz each) tomato
    sauce
¼ c pure water

Combine meat, sauerkraut, onion, egg, brown rice, caraway seeds, kelp & herbs; mix lightly. Trim thickest part of stem from cabbage leaves. Divide meat into 12 equal portions and place one on each cabbage leaf. Roll leaves around meat, tucking ends as you roll; then fasten with wooden picks. Brown rolls lightly in oil. Add tomato sauce and water. Cover and cook slowly in skillet, or moderate oven (350°F.) 40 minutes or until cabbage is tender. *Serves 4.*

VARIATION: You may place a layer of canned sauerkraut under cabbage rolls.

BOILED BRISKET WITH SAUERKRAUT

4 lbs well-trimmed double
    brisket of beef
4 c salt-free sauerkraut

1 tbsp honey
1 tbsp caraway seeds
2 tbsp whole wheat flour

1 large grated raw potato

Use choice quality meat. Mix sauerkraut, potato, honey, and caraway seeds. Place half in a heavy 4 quart saucepan. Put meat on this, and cover with the remaining sauerkraut mixture. If sauerkraut is dry, add ½ cup water. Cover, bring to a boil, then lower heat and simmer about 3½ hours, until the meat is very tender. Mix flour to a smooth paste with a little cold water and add. Cook gently for 5 minutes. Serve meat on a platter and sauerkraut in a separate bowl. *Serves 8.*

SAUERKRAUT SANDWICHES

HERCULEAN KRAUTWICHES

Everybody loves a hero! There's no better way to banish he-man hungers than with a super colossal, double delectable hero sandwich. Brimful of tangy fixings, these jaw-stretchers come in all shapes and sizes and they're crowned with tart, springy kraut at its best. If you're planning a backyard bash, turning teens loose in the kitchen or looking for a Sunday supper menu, why not set out a tray of cold chicken, turkey, beef or lamb cuts and cheeses; sliced onion, tomato, cucumber and green pepper and lettuce; plus a selection of health bread and rolls. Let everyone create his own concoction. And don't forget a big bowl of crisp, pungent kraut to top off the jumbo sandwiches. Kraut and cold meats are an unbeatable combination.

HEALTH REUBEN KRAUTWICH

The Reuben has taken the country by storm. Now you can serve this succulent grilled combo of vegeburger*, Swiss cheese and kraut on rye at home.

2 c drained salt-free sauerkraut	½ tsp caraway or dill seed
	¼ tsp garlic powder
16 slices rye bread	½ c Russian dressing
1 lb cooked vegeburger	1 lb sliced Swiss cheese

Melted salt-free butter or soy oil

**Conventional meat eaters would add corned beef.*

Toss kraut with caraway seed and garlic powder; set aside. Spread bread with dressing. Top 8 slices bread with sliced vegeburger, kraut, cheese and remaining bread. Brush melted butter on both sides of sandwiches. Grill in skillet or electric sandwich toaster until cheese is melted.

53

TWO HEROES ITALIAN STYLE

Twin heroes from one round loaf. The flavor is deliciously pizza.

7-inch round loaf of
hearth rye bread
2 c well-drained salt-free
sauerkraut
½ tsp kelp seasoning
½ lb sliced, cooked turkey,
chicken, beef, or lamb

12 oz mozzarella cheese,
shredded
½ can (3 oz) tomato paste
1½ tsp oregano leaves
dash of Italian herbs
⅓ lb sliced assorted cheeses

Cut bread into 5 horizontal slices. Sprinkle remaining slices with about ½ of the cheese. Mix kraut, tomato paste and seasonings. On each bread slice, layer about ½ cup of kraut mixture, ¼ of the turkey, chicken, etc. and assorted cheeses; sprinkle with remaining cheese. Stack 2 slices for each hero and wrap in foil. Heat in a 400⁰ (hot) oven 35 minutes; open foil and heat 10 minutes longer to brown cheese lightly. Cut in wedges and serve. *Serves 8.*

ROTUND HEROES

4 c well-drained salt-free
sauerkraut
1 medium cucumber, pared
and thinly sliced (1 c)
Butter or soy oil
lettuce
4 rectangular slices Swiss
cheese, halved

Russian dressing
¼ c chopped parsley
kelp seasoning
1 round loaf of rye bread,
7 to 8 inches in diameter
¾ lb sliced turkey or
chicken, etc.
1 jar (4 oz) pimiento,
drained and split

Toss and chill: kraut, dressing and parsley. Season cucumbers with kelp seasoning.

Cut bread horizontally into 6 slices. Lightly butter each slice. For each hero, use 3 slices bread and assemble simultaneously on 2 separate plates. Layer first with lettuce, ¼ of the kraut mixture, ½ the turkey an cheese. Add second slice of bread and layers of lettuce, remaining kraut mixture, cucumber and pimiento. Top with third slice. Wrap and chill heroes 2 to 3 hours before serving. Cut into wedges. *Makes 2 large heroes, about 12 servings.*

BE A CHINESE HERO KRAUTWICH

'Tis a bit messy to eat, but the flavor makes it well worthwhile.

½ package (8 oz) fresh or
frozen Chinese pea pods
1 can (5 oz) water chestnuts,
drained and sliced
1 lb sliced chicken loaf
amino acids (soy sauce)

4 c well-drained salt-free
sauerkraut
Health Mayonnaise
6 hero wholewheat or bread
rolls, 6-inches long, split

Drop pea pods in boiling water for 1 minute. Drain well and toss with kraut, water chestnuts and 2/3 cup mayonnaise; chill. Spread both halves of rolls with mayonnaise. Brush chicken slices with soy sauce. Assemble each sandwich with a layer of kraut mixture and sliced chicken. *Makes 6 sandwiches.*

THE JOLLY DUTCHMAN
TRIPLE DECKER

3 packages (3 oz each)
cream cheese
18 slices pumpernickel
bread (about 1 medium
loaf)

2 tbsp chopped chives
2 c well-drained salt-free
sauerkraut
butter or unsaturated oil
6 slices of chicken or turkey

Blend thoroughly 3 ounces cream cheese and 1 tablespoon chives. Stir in kraut and chill. In medium bowl blend together remaining cream cheese and chives.

Using 3 slices of bread for each sandwich, assemble as follows: On the first slice spread 1/3 cup of the kraut mixture. On second slice spread 2 tablespoons of the cheese mixture and add several slices of chicken or turkey. Butter remaining slices and top sandwiches. *Makes 6 sandwiches.*

LORD NELSON HERO

15-inch loaf of Italian rye
bread, cut in half lengthwise
1 medium chopped tomato
¼ c chopped scallion
1 clove crushed garlic
kelp, seasoning to taste
1 lb sliced cheddar cheese,
cut in strips

Softened butter or olive
oil
2 c well-drained salt-free
sauerkraut
½ c each: diced green
pepper, chopped olives
¼ c Health Mayonnaise

Remove soft center from each half of bread*, leaving crust wall 1-inch thick. Lightly butter each half.

Combine kraut, vegetables, olives, garlic and seasonings; pack into top half of bread. Toss cheese with mayonnaise and pack into bottom half. Press halves together lightly and wrap tightly in foil. Chill several hours. Slice to serve. *Serves 6 to 8.*
Use soft center for bread crumbs in stuffings, etc.

HEROES LOVE A HERO KRAUTWICH

2 c well-drained salt-free
sauerkraut
¼ tsp dill weed
Romaine lettuce
4 slices sweet onion
½ lb sliced turkey or
chicken
½ lb sliced lamb or beef

½ c sour cream
1 tbsp chopped chives
15-inch loaf of Italian rye
bread, halved lengthwise
and buttered
3 large rectangular slices
Swiss cheese, halved
1 thinly sliced tomato

Mix kraut with sour cream, chives and dill weed; chill. On bottom half of bread, layer: lettuce, onion, cheese, tomato, then kraut mixture. Cover with top of bread. Secure with picks. *Serves 6 to 8.*

THE POWER OF HEALTH PIZZA

The noble pizza in all its glory, brims with mushrooms, cheese and soul-satisfying sauerkraut.

1 package (13¾ oz) whole
  wheat hot roll mix
2 c drained salt-free
  sauerkraut
¼ tsp basil leaves
½ lb sliced mozzarella
  cheese

Olive or safflower oil
1 small onion, chopped
2 cans (8 oz each) tomato
  sauce
6 to 8 green pepper rings
1 c fresh sliced mushrooms
  grated Parmesan cheese

Prepare hot roll mix as directed on package for pizza dough. Pat out half the dough in a 14-inch pizza pan; freeze remainder for later use*. Brush lightly with oil. Brown onion in skillet. Add kraut, tomato sauce and basil; stir and heat. Spread kraut mixture over pizza dough. Top with green pepper and mozzarella cheese. Sprinkle with Parmesan cheese. Bake in 450⁰ (very hot) oven 15 to 20 minutes. *Makes a 14-inch pie.*
If desired, prepare 2 pizzas, doubling the filling ingredients.

Let food be your medicine, and medicine be your food. —Hippocrates

---

The best service a book can render is to impart truth, but to make you think it out for yourself.   —Elbert Hubbard

---

To preserve health is a moral and religious duty, for health is the basis for all social virtues. We can no longer be useful when not well.
                              —Dr. Samuel Johnson, Father of Dictionaries

TEN HEALTH COMMANDMENTS

Thou shall respect thy body as the highest manifestation of Life.

Thou shall abstain from all unnatural, devitalized food and stimulating beverages.

Thou shall nourish thy body with only Natural, unprocessed, "live" food, —that

Thou shall extend thy years in health for loving, charitable service.

Thou shall regenerate thy body by the right balance of activity and rest.

Thou shall purify thy cells, tissue and blood with pure fresh air and sunshine.

Thou shall abstain from ALL food when out of sorts in mind or body.

Thou shall keep thy thoughts, words and emotions, pure, calm and uplifting.

Thou shall increase thy knowledge of Nature's laws, abide therewith, and enjoy the fruits of thy life's labor.

Thou shall lift up thyself and thy brother man with thine own obedience to ALL Nature's laws.

IS YOUR BIRTHRIGHT
HEALTH
CULTIVATE IT

FROM THE AUTHORS

This book was written for YOU. It can be your passport to the Good Life. We Professional Nutritionists join hands in one common objective — a high standard of health for all and many added years to your life. Scientific Nutrition points the way — Nature's Way — the only lasting way to build a body free of degenerative diseases and premature aging. This book teaches you how to work with Nature and not against her. Doctors, dentists, and others who care for the sick, try to repair depleted tissues which too often mend poorly if at all. Many of them praise the spreading of this new scientific message of natural foods and methods for long-lasting health and youthfulness at any age. To speed the spreading of this tremendous message, this book was written.

Statements in this book are recitals of scientific findings, known facts of physiology, biological therapeutics, and reference to ancient writings as they are found. Paul C. Bragg has been practicing the natural methods of living for over 70 years, with highly beneficial results, knowing they are safe and of great value to others, and his daughter Patricia Bragg works with him to carry on the Health Crusade. They make no claims as to what the methods cited in this book will do for one in any given situation, and assume no obligation because of opinions expressed.

No cure for disease is offered in this book. No foods or diets are offered for the treatment or cure of any specific ailment. Nor is it intended as, or to be used as, literature for any food product. Paul C. Bragg and Patricia Bragg express their opinions solely as Public Health Educators, Professional Nutritionists and Teachers.

Certain persons considered experts may disagree with one or more statements in this book, as the same relate to various nutritional recommendations. However, any such statements are considered, nevertheless, to be factual, as based upon long-time experience of Paul C. Bragg and Patricia Bragg in the field of human health.

WE THANK THEE

For flowers that bloom about our feet;
    For song of bird and hum of bee;
For all things fair we hear or see,
    Father in heaven we thank Thee!
For blue of stream and blue of sky;
    For pleasant shade of branches high;
For fragrant air and cooling breeze;
    For beauty of the blooming trees,
Father in heaven, we thank Thee!
    For mother-love and father-care,
For brothers strong and sisters fair;
    For love at home and here each day;
For guidance lest we go astray,
    Father in heaven, we thank Thee!
For this new morning with its light;
    For rest and shelter of the night;
For health and food, for love and friends;
    For every thing His goodness sends,
Father in heaven, we thank Thee!

               – Ralph Waldo Emerson

MY FAVORITE
SAUERKRAUT RECIPES

INGREDIENTS

Salt-Free Sauerkraut

MY FAVORITE
SAUERKRAUT RECIPES

INGREDIENTS

BRAGG
Live Longer, Live Stronger
Self-Improvement
LIBRARY

Let These Amazing Health Books Show You, Your Family And Friends The Road To Health, Happiness And A Long, Vital Life! Each Of These Books Is A Priceless And Valuable Treasure To Help Safeguard Your Health.

Please send Free Health Bulletins to these friends and relatives:

Name

Address

City   State   Zip Code

Name

Address

City   State   Zip Code

Name

Address

City   State   Zip Code

Name

Address

City   State   Zip Code

Name

Address

City   State   Zip Code

Name

Address

City   State   Zip Code

PLEASE CUT ALONG DOTTED LINE

PATRICIA BRAGG, Ph.D.

Nutritionist, Beauty and Health Consultant

Advisor to World Leaders, Glamorous Hollywood Stars, Singers, Dancers, Athletes

LECTURER and AUTHOR

Daughter of the world renowned health authority, Paul C. Bragg, Patricia Bragg has won international fame on her own in this field. She conducts Health and Fitness Seminars for women's, men's, youth and church groups throughout the United States . . . and is co-lecturer with Paul C. Bragg on tours throughout the English speaking world. Consultants to Presidents and Royalty, to Stars of Stage, Screen and TV, and to Champion Athletes, Patricia Bragg and her father are authors and co-authors of the Bragg Health Library of instructive, inspiring books.

Patricia Bragg herself is the symbol of perpetual youth, a living and sparkling example of hers and her father's precepts.

A fifth generation Californian on her mother's side, Patricia Bragg was reared by the Natural Health Method from infancy. In school, she not only excelled in athletics but also won high honors in her studies and her counseling. She is an accomplished musician and dancer . . . as well as tennis player, swimmer and mountain climber . . . and the youngest woman ever to be granted a U.S. Patent. An alumna of the University of California, and recently earning a Ph.D. in Health Sciences, Patricia Bragg is a popular and gifted Health Teacher.

She has been Health Consultant to that great walker, President Harry S. Truman, and to the British Royal Family.

Betty Cuthbert, Australia's "Golden Girl" who holds 16 world's records and 4 Olympic gold medals in women's track, follows Patricia Bragg's guidance. Among those who come to Patricia Bragg for advice are Clint and Maggie Eastwood, Connie Haines, Pamela Mason, Joe Feeney (singing star of Lawrence Welk's TV show) and his family of nine children, and Marilyn Van Derbur, the former Miss America who is now a famous TV personality, speaker and teacher. Patricia Bragg has helped many other official "Miss and Mr. Americas" . . . plus many thousands of unofficial Mr. and Ms. Americas and their families who read her books and attend her lectures.

Dear friend, I wish above all things that thou may prosper and be in health even as the soul prosper—3 John:2

Ps. 23:1–3, 2 Cor. 5:17, Matt. 8:7, Prov. 3:17, Isa. 40:31